This is the third book in a series titled "Stories You and I Want to Tell."

Upon completing Volume 2, I had some material leftover which I decided to put into a third volume. I added a few more and the foregoing is the result. Additionally, these are not only stories here, but memories, essays, musings, and thoughts on various subjects. It has a little bit of everything and a lot of nothing. Just a collection of different subjects. Thus, the title "Leftover Stories." I sincerely hope my family and friends will find this little book enjoyable.

Stories – Some Leftover

By

Eddie Dean

A collection of stories, essays, thoughts, musings and other

trivia, including thoughts and memories of bygone friends.

Written by: Eddie Dean – Revised and edited by: Jeremiah Dean 2018

A Robbery in Booneville

The big, late model Packard edged its way down the winding hill. It was approaching the Kentucky River bridge near Beattyville. The driver was operating in such a careful manner so as not to draw attention to the vehicle or its occupants. On the back of the car the out of county tags were stolen, and under the driver's seat were three extra sets. Those sets were for interchanging on occasions, and like the ones on the car, they too were stolen.

Upon making a curve at the foot of that hill, the driver's eyes beheld a roadblock of local police, and he knew a tinge of fear as he realized that his journey was ending and the game was over. The three men inside were all black men. Their names were Carl Lewis, Thurman Maley, and James Roberts, and all were from Cincinnati. Upon being taken into custody, there must have been some apprehension felt, as they were quickly taken back to Owsley County, an area that, along with its surrounding counties were predominantly all white.

The three were fleeing from a crime that they had committed a short time before, near Booneville. Each of them was familiar with the ritual of being arrested, as they were all ex-convicts. The next day was January the 5th, 1955 and I was nine years old. We lived in a rural area of Upper Buffalo in Owsley County.

My father was a deputy sheriff, and I recall the big black sedan that came creeping up the creek bed to our house. Some men got out and told him he was badly needed in town to help guard the jail. The town was filled with several hundred people and it was not a festive crowd. As a matter of fact, there was a lot of talk about lynching.

Even though 1955 was not that long ago in history, the possibility of such a thing happening was very real in those days. In some rural areas of the South, not only was it a possibility, but a few times did occur.

My father piled into that big car and headed out with its occupants to see justice take its lawful course. Even though hundreds milled around town and voices were raised in anger, the cooler heads prevailed and violence did not take root. In a day or so the citizens had settled down and the entire episode was handled lawfully.

All this activity had taken place because these three black men had beaten and robbed an elderly lady by the name of Susie Wilson, whom local rumors held, always had a large sum of money on hand. She had been bound and beaten by the trio until she told where her stash was hidden. Entrance to her home had been by force. When captured the sum total of money recovered was 875.00. Much less than what the robbers had been told to expect. They had been told that the Wilsons kept as much as 50,000 dollars on hand.

In a matter of three or four weeks two other arrest would be made in far Northern Kentucky. Those taken into custody had been snitched out by the suspects, and both of those recent arrests were white men. They were 37-year-old Howard Flynn and 36-year-old George Hoar. One of the pair had come to Booneville previously to point out the Wilson home to the robbers. I don't know, but would guess that one or both of the two had Owsley connections, or they would not have been privy to the rumors about Susie Wilson hording up cash.

Over the years I have heard different stories about this affair and most are different in some degree from the way I have told it. I Have recreated it from old newspaper accounts of the incident and quotes attributed to Owsley County Judge Seales. Lawyers, and others in law enforcement during those mid fifty years. However, the outcome of the trials settling the affair, I have been unable to establish. I think that may be because the courthouse burned some years later, and a lot of records were lost. I am sure that there are many, like myself, who were kids and can recall the excitement of this event. Some of those that still live may recall the outcome of those follow up trials.

The Pool Room

When one is young, they often learn a lot about human nature by their observations of others. In my case, a lot was gained through interactions and observations with family and extended family. Cousins, nephews, aunts, uncles, along with brothers and sisters were more prominent in my education, as those were the ones I spent the most time around. School would of course have to be second as it was there that I spent a third of my young life. There would be very few of us that cannot recall a teacher or student that did not have some influence upon the way we would think or act.

In many cases though, especially when I started into my younger teen years, I learned about the complexities of humanity from places far different than those mentioned above. I have talked before about the little country stores and the colorful figures that concentrated there. One could learn a lot from the characters that assembled and hung out in those social centers of yesterday. However, I think for pure analytical and psychological studies, one could never beat the community pool rooms. The long, gone pool halls of the fifties and sixties were a place where one was exposed to the most basic principles of humanity. In those days every little town or village had a pool room, and they were for many years the busiest places in town. The pool rooms were a male dominated cultural center and girls nor women, as a rule, did not enter therein.

These pool halls, like the country stores are now gone. They were a place of bravado, where the young men discussed who had the fastest car, the best job or the best-looking girlfriends. It was also a place where many young men bragged about his latest sexual conquest. (Which in many cases were fabricated. A few young maidens achieved a less than favorable reputation because of pool room conversation. Reputations, which in many cases were unwarranted).

In the late fifties and early sixties my father ran Mark Dean's pool room in Oneida. During summer months and weekends, I could often be found hanging out with him while he hustled around racking and collecting fees from the tables. It was here that I watched with wide eyes, the exchange of greenbacks after each and every game. The losers would grudgingly pull forth from their pockets what was then, scarce and hard to come by dollars.

Not all the games played were for money, but there was, in every pool room, that one table that was primarily set aside for those that favored that game of chance. It was almost always ringed with several individuals with serious and intense looks as they stalked around the table and constantly chalked their cues.

Then there were the twelve and thirteen-year old's, like myself, who watched in awe as the best in town taunted and jostled each other around that velvet covered table. Our eyes bogged at the exchange of coins which clanged loudly as they were tossed on the table, to be gathered up by the winner after every game. Coins that we did not possess, and could not conceive of discarding so lightly, even if we did. Everything about that table bespoke money. The table itself was manufactured in an expensive way, and covered in soft plush green velvet. Along the sides the rails were inlaid with ivory. Even the players around it took on expensive air's as they strutted and put on a show for the observers.

Most of us young kids wanted to be like them, and maybe even become a pool shark, or pro when we grew up, and have money to splurge. We secretly worshiped some of those local pros who so brilliantly displayed their skills. The action was a grand display of life itself, staged at a minuscule level. The pool room life was fascinating to our young adolescent minds.

Then, sometime in 1961 a young fellow who frequented Taylor's Pool Hall, in Richmond gave the world a book. His name was Walter Tevis, and though he was a highly educated individual, he could often be found doing a little pool hustling himself in those billiard parlors around central Kentucky. The book was titled "The Hustler" and came to the attention of Hollywood, which in turn saw it evolve into a movie. With a stellar cast consisting of Jackie Gleason, Paul Newman, George C Scott and other high-profile stars.

The Hustler was a hit and still has a cult following. Following that movie, those local pros in all the little towns immediately took notice, and it seemed their pride and haughty personalities increased ten-fold. Of course, us young hanger-on's viewed them with much more esteem as well. Mr. Tevis and his book brought the pool room business to the forefront of America's attention. For the next several years pool was America's great male pastime and entering a billiard hall one was hard pressed to find an available table not in use.

There were several decent pool players I recall from the days of Dean's Pool Room. I will mention a few that I thought played well, though only one or two of those I think could have made the professional circuit that existed back in the heyday of billiards. Bob Webb comes to mind quickest, probably because he was just a few years older than me, and later he and I would become good friends. Bob lived high on the Sandlin Hill, near Oneida. He would walk to town a couple of times every day to check out the action. Donald Jean Burns lived near Bob, and he too was a frequent player on the money table.

Then there was an infrequent guest named Garnett Davidson who was probably as close to a pro as there was in the gambling circuit. Garnett's entire life was dedicated to gambling, but even though he played decent pool, cards was what he was most adept to. If you saw him playing pool, you could rest assured that there were no poker games anywhere at that present time. He often played high stakes poker in far off places like Cincinnati. Like all gamblers, Garnett's life was a road of highs and lows as it related to income. Generally speaking though, he shot a decent stick when he had to lower himself to the pool circuit.

Bob Webb was, as mentioned, nearer to my age, and was very young to be as good as he was. He went off to Vietnam before I did, and survived his tour as a gunner on one of those old antique Huey's. He came home, and in a year or so died in an alcohol related car wreck. Bob was good on the table and was always seeking to play a little check pool. He often would win a little, but for the most part, his first hour or so was his highlight. Bob's problem was, he could not tolerate any faults or failure on his part. He was a dynamo with the balls, until at some point, he would miss, or make a slight

miscalculation and his anger would arise. When that happened, his skill disappeared, and for the rest of that day would not return. Once mad at himself, that beautiful artistry went away and it would be the next day before he could recapture it.

Donald Jean played well enough, but he too suffered from Bob's ailment. However, Donald Jean did not get angry at himself. His was more directed at the games principals. There was an old maxim related to playing pool known as "talking one out of his shots." Those fellow players learned early that herein lay Donald's weakness. When he leaned over the table for that high stakes shop, those opponents would jokingly start on him. Kidding, verbally badgering and teasing. This would generally distract him, or cause him to become upset, and as a result, he would blow that important shot. Once that happened, like Bob, his grace was laid to rest for that day.

The best around Dean's Pool Room, was no doubt Doug Treadway. Doug possessed what the Hustler did. For those locals that played with him, they pretty much generally lost. He was slow, methodical and precise. He flowed around the table with ease. His entire attention always seemed focused on those balls, and he became oblivious to everything and everybody around. Verbal comments, jokes, and badgering had no effect whatever. When he got that one open shot, it was pretty well over, no matter how many balls he had to run. He shot for position and was very good at it. As a young fellow, I remember Doug as being the closest thing to a pro that we had.

There were a few others, but those aforementioned folks are some that come to mind. What did I learn about human nature at the pool room? Well, for one, I learned that you must possess certain traits to fit into any profession you chose in life. I also learned that I could not shoot pool nor would I ever. I did not possess those traits that were required.

However, I did learn some lessons that pointed out things that were needed to maintain an even keel in life. Of those, persistent, calmness and control in times of personal upheaval figured very importantly in one's life. Another important lesson was to keep cool in relationships with others, go slow and don't over heat or fret about mistakes you make. Just take a deep breath and know your momentum will generally return upon the morrow.

I guess the one trait I learned that served me well was that of patience. With patience, there are few obstacles that can't be overcome. To be truthful though, there were a lot of lessons learned that I seldom practiced, and if I had stayed focused on those pool room events my life might have run a much smoother course.

The Kelly Files

Sometimes one sees and hears things that are unexplainable. When such an event happens it often dwells on your mind for days. That is how an event a few weeks back affected me. It was late evening hours and darkness had settled over the hills and valleys. I had to make an excursion outside to retrieve my phone from the truck, and as always, I had to glance skyward. It was a cloudless sky I saw, and as always, far removed from the artificial lights of man, the Heavens shown their brilliancy. I had to stop and study the immense number of stars for a moment. It was during this brief moment of looking Heavenly that I saw something I had never seen before. It shot from over the horizon and appeared to be a star itself.

My first thought was what we referred to as kids, a shooting star, or maybe a comet. I had no time to reflect then, as my thoughts could not keep pace with the speed of this light. The amazing thing was that when it reached mid sky, it instantly reversed itself and shot back on the same path and over the horizon from where it originally appeared. It did not stop or hesitate, but simply reversed. The speed as mentioned was incredibly fast. The entire sighting took just a few seconds. The next few days I kept thinking back to the incident and even mentioned it to a few people. Not one I talked to about it had seen anything of this nature. Though many stated that they had seen man made satellites that appeared as I described, but they always went horizon to horizon. No one had seen one reverse itself, nor did they move with great speed, but fairly slowly across the sky.

I finally decided that maybe I was looking for answers in the wrong place. Maybe what I had observed fell under the category of unknown Phenomenon. Maybe what I saw was a UFO. It would be my first, and I certainly had never saw any Heavenly body react in this manner. It was with this thought in mind that I decided to do research and find out about objects others had spotted that may have acted in this fashion. Living in the modern age, I did what most do. I simply went to Google. Going through various UFO sightings, I found out this was pretty common with UFO's. Right and left turns, 45-degree, 90-degree, reverse, high speeds - all those were well documented.

Once I got into the research, I began reading a lot of material that had nothing to do with my original quest. It was then that I discovered that one of the more fantastic UFO encounters was in my home state of Kentucky. It's known as the Kelly Files and occurred in a little farming community by the same name. There were two families dwelling in an old farmhouse far remote, and out in the country. Another local farmer informed them he had seen a glowing object make a landing behind their house. The house mentioned had two husband and wife couples and several kids. This was in the mid-fifties and there was no phone service available to those remote individuals.

The way the story goes they were kept inside all night by little, elf looking creatures, with long arms and legs, with big eyes and large heads. Their skin or maybe tight-fitting suits were silver in color and they themselves, were at the most four feet tall. One of the men finally got up enough nerve to venture to the front porch and confront the subjects, but a long arm came down from the roof of the porch and grabbed him by the hair, then attempted to pull him upward. His nerve then broke, he escaped, minus some hair, and reentered the house quickly. The rest of the night the creatures showed themselves at the windows trying to seek entrance, and also at the doors. Having firearms, the men shot several rounds at the little guys, but shots had no effect whatsoever.

With daylight, the Aliens departed, and all the families piled into two vehicles and went to their local Sheriff's department. Before the day was over more than twenty Law Enforcement officers were on the farm looking for evidence. Three of these were Military Police, which I found a little odd. The only damage encountered was that caused by the firing of shots by those residing in the house. The first thing I thought about was maybe alcohol and drugs, but every police officer ruled that out. All reports stated that the folks were in a high state of hysteria and frightened beyond belief. Alcohol and drugs were the first things ruled out. One Sheriff went so far as to say he was not surprised, as he had seen strange objects himself in the previous few weeks.

The story of the little men was picked up by the press and carried near and far across America. Not too many years in the future, a young Movie director, who had some success under his belt already, stumbled across the story. He had been thinking along the line of making a few movies using the "Alien" theme, and the old Newspaper reports sent him to digging. After researching the Kelly Episode and talking to some of those involved, he was intrigued enough to make two movies. One of those has always been one of my favorites. That one being, "Close Encounters of The Third Kind." Another movie would be based on the physical descriptions of those little farm Invaders, and we all know it as "ET ".

We all know those movies, but what we did not know, was that an Alien encounter in my home state of Kentucky, had a lot to do with their production. I really don't know what any of this has to do with my UFO sighting, but as I often do, I have gotten off track. That's not conducive to good writing, but for storytelling, its allowed and OK.

I am at the old Mountain Cabin as I write this, it's late night and the weather is warm. I have my windows open, and for several minutes, there has been a sound like a cat scratching on the screens. My storm doors are locked, but there is also a noise as if something or someone is jiggling and trying to open.

There is no wind tonight, and the sky is cloudy. Outside its very dark. I best close this UFO story now, as I must go investigate these strange noises. If you don't hear from me for a few weeks, try and look towards the night skies occasionally. I might be trying to phone home.

The Night the Devil Stopped the Lord's Work

There is a lot of entertainment available today. Most everyone can find ways of keeping their minds and bodies occupied. It was not always this way, and any local events that cropped up were heavily attended. This applied even more so in the rural and remote areas of eastern Kentucky. Such events as Revival meetings, church gatherings, dances and other happenings would draw in large crowds. The Revival Meetings alone would last for days or weeks, and folks would travel from great distances to attend. It was an event where they could socialize. An event whereby they could escape the everyday boredom and drudgery of the hardworking life that faced them daily. Those revival meetings often had the biggest crowds. Granted, not everyone came for worship. Many had ulterior motives for making those long trips by horse, buggies, or walking, and the few automobiles that were then in use.

Many of the young people showed up seeking companionship and attention with other young of the opposite sex. Romance was their reasoning. There were others, primarily males, who came to sip their shine, mingle, and just hang out. They stayed outside and away from the indoor believers. Sometimes that demon shine would push a few over the edge, and fights and scuffles would break out. While the God of peace often reigned inside, the Devil himself often jostled and wrestled with those outside. We can probably assume that seventy percent were there for worship, the rest, for other reasons.

The period in time that I am speaking of would be mostly the thirties, forties, and to a lesser degree, into the fifties. It was those years when the Holy Roller religion was at its peak, with the forties being more prominent. It was also the thirties and forties when the popularity of handling snakes spread rapidly throughout East Kentucky and the other states of the Appalachian chain. With that thought in mind, we can also guess that a sizable portion of those in attendance at these revivals were curious, or there to observe the dangerous practice of handling the serpents. The state legislature finally chose to intervene, and in 1946 they created a law making it a crime. This had little effect, and was seldom prosecuted, so the practice continued well into the fifties, at which time it started diminishing somewhat.

However, even today one will sometimes hear news reports of someone dying or suffering from a snake bite in some Kentucky religious event. I recall myself at some of those ceremonies in the fifties when I, along with other young friends, would drop into a little church beside Mark Deans pool room. Our purpose was to stare and glare at this strange and fearful practice. I can still visualize the jumping, shouting, and passing of the slithering serpents, from one hand to another. The biggest rattlesnakes I saw in my lifetime, I saw in that little Church. They often appeared to a little boy to be the size of a grown man's arm, and some probably were. So, it was that snake handling had become a way to prove, and or, show your faith in those hard years before, during and after WWII.

It had spread rapidly and by 1940 had a large following in Owsley County Kentucky. It was there, in the early part of 1940, that a snake handling ritual turned into a murder scene. It was a mild weather day, and several men had used it to erect a large tent. The location of the tent was in a little creek bottom near the Lerose, post office, just a few miles from the county seat of Booneville. Even though it was a large tent, it was not large enough to handle the unexpected crowd of more than three hundred people that starting drifting in. The preacher's decided at the start of the service to roll two sides of the tent up to accommodate those outside who could not gain entrance.

One of the preachers that night was FD Amburgey. On the rough plank platform with FD was his son, seventeen-year-old Kash. Kash was a believer and he was there to handle the snakes also. That was not that unusual, as the children who felt they had the faith and the belief to do, as did the adults, were in many cases, allowed to do so. They were also allowed to testify. Young Kash Amburgey had the misfortune that night to see his faith severely tested. His serpent nailed him immediately on his thumb. He attempted to continue with the service but in just a matter of minutes he became so gravely ill that his mother removed him and took him home. I have never found out if a doctor was called or not. However, his father remained and continued to preach at the service.

Outside, at the time Kash was bitten, was one Cuda Amburgey. Cuda was FD's brother, thus he was Kash's Uncle. However, he was not there to worship, but was in attendance with some other friends and family members to sip a little shine, and just to congregate. Cuda thought highly of his young nephew, and when the news came out into the yard that Kash had suffered a bite, he became enraged and belligerent. Already under the influence he drew his pistol and charged into the tent and headed towards the stage yelling that he was going to kill every one of those G.. D.. snakes.

A deputy sheriff by the name of Hayes Estep was in attendance, and he, along with some others, got Cuda wrestled down and removed back outside. In a few moments friends persuaded him to leave and he did. The problem was he did not stay gone but returned in about thirty minutes, still mad......still drinking, and still pulling his gun and swearing. He would later testify that he had only drank one pint of shine that evening. It was only a short time after his return, that the outside darkness was shattered by three shots. Confusion reigned, and some said the shots came from the back, some from the front, and others speculated even from the rear. A few said they came from where Cuda was standing. Regardless those shots had been fired in the direction of the stage. Though probably unintentionally, one of those shots hit a serpent handler by the name of Arco Angel. Arco did not have to fear the snakes, or prove his faith. His death was pretty much instant.

Strange as it seems, there was no arrest or investigation. The matter was to linger for four months, at which time a Grand Jury took up the matter and began looking into it. Theirs was the only investigation, and it centered on the testimony of witnesses. Regardless, an indictment was returned and the case went to trial. Cuda's defense called 27 witnesses, the Commonwealth called 22. With all the witnesses called, only one turned out to be a definite for the prosecution, and that was a thirteen-year-old boy by the name of Junior McIntosh. He was the one person that said he saw Cuda raise his gun and aim towards the stage and fire. One of the things that I find amazing about this crime was how, in a crowd of hundreds, could one-man fire and only be seen by one small boy.

I have also wondered if the little community of Lerose had any electricity in the early forties. I doubt it, and if they did not, the outside and away from the stage would have been very dark. What light would have been available, would have been kerosene and that only in the stage area inside. There were reports and testimonials about powder flashes, but everyone had differing opinions about where they came from. Regardless, Cuda Amburgey was only found guilty of manslaughter and had a very lenient sentence imposed. That sentence being two years behind bars. He chooses to appeal and a lengthy appeal process then followed. The court would uphold his sentence

Reading the court's decision, one would think that they held up the conviction more from the Defendant's actions on the evening in question, than they did with any of the points brought up during the trial. It was pointed out by the court that numerous people had seen him flashing his pistol that night. They also pointed out that the Deputy Sheriff had requested his gun immediately after the shots were fired as he was being hustled off the scene by his drinking friends and some of his relatives. His reply was that he had no gun, and he had given it to Redvine, a family member. No one would produce the gun, nor did the gun ever show up. The Court stated that the deputy's inspection of the gun could well have been proven if it had just been fired, thus proving his innocence or guilt on the spot. In other words, they felt that the way the gun issue was handled indicated guilt.

I had heard the stories about this event for many years, but it was only recently that I read the actual court records. The thoughts, facts ,etc reproduced here, came from those records. When I was around the Southern Ohio area during the late sixties or maybe early seventies, the TV airways were filled with a commercial starring a man with a big hat. The words of the commercial were delivered in a slow mountain drawl whereby he would Invite you to "Come to Kash's Big Bargain Barn." Where you would save Cash with Kash. I did not know then, that this was the Kash that had received that snake bite which caused a killing those many years ago. A few people probably knew the entire story on what happened that night, but there were so many conflicting tales from the witnesses produced that there would have always been doubt, no matter what the outcome would have been.

One Witness, when asked about what went on at that service, pretty much summed it up. "The Devil Wouldn't let the Lord Work That Night," he said. In defense of the snake handlers, I guess one could repeat St Mark: 16;18. "They shall take up serpents, and if they drink any deadly thing, it shall not hurt them" or Luke put it another way, "Behold, I give you power to tread on Serpents and scorpions" I personally think the Biblical Words, "Do not temp the Lord thy God" applies more in my case.

Sickness and Old Times

It's the last part of January, 2016. Kentucky is just thawing out from a record-breaking snowstorm. Me. Well, I have been trying to deal with the most excruciating tooth pain that I've ever had. Can't get it pulled because it's infected. So, I am shut-in, trying to keep my mind in a positive mode, and eating ibuprofen.

Being indoors for a few days is itself enough to keep a body down, and causes one's mind to conjure up thoughts and images of other places and times. I did get to the local pharmacy and picked up some medications to fight the infection. There are dozens of pharmacies around town and they all seem to be quite booming businesses. On the way home, I got my mind on the old days. There was severe pain, sickness, depression, etc. back then too. Even though I have to say, I believe it was on a much smaller scale than today.

My father lived to be 78, and he had only one or two teeth left when he died. Now, he must have had some severe toothache pain, but he never went to the dentist. Where did his teeth go? Did someone pull them for him or did he work them out himself?

An abscessed tooth can kill one today if you don't get it pulled. Just generally bad teeth themselves can cause problems elsewhere. Then there were broken bones, flu epidemics, from which many died, and some terrible painful and killing illnesses for which there were no specialists or doctors to consult with. I got to thinking that the good old days, we sometimes think about, were horrendous times for many. It would have been a great life, but when human ills and the pain came it could have been a nightmare.

I recalled that when I was a child in the early fifties, the medical treatments on Buffalo were pretty consistent with what they had been for a century or two. I don't recall a lot of sickness in the population but maybe being a child, I did not take note. But I have searched my mind and what few instances of sickness that come to mind were mostly the elderly. It seemed they got old, ended up bed fast, then death followed fairly quickly. The younger population seemed to recover well from mishaps and the maladies of the day. I do recall seeing a few at one time or another with a poultice placed on their head or jaw for tooth aches and headaches. I kind of wished I knew what was in those little rag wrapped bandages. A few days back I'd sure have attempted one on my toothache since the pain came creeping in the late-night hours.

Then there were a few deaths from drinking that old mountain shine, but it wasn't from the shine itself, but rather companion drinkers whose brains were inflamed by the liquor that dealt the final blow. Mountain moonshine seems to have brought out a vicious hatred and disregard for life, from some of the community's most meek and humble citizens. I suppose it was the drug problem of that day.

Anyway, dwelling on medications of the time, they were simply not available. The medicine that pulled people through came from nature. The Woods were their medicine cabinet and it was from there that they collected and stored a various collection of assorted barks, herbs, roots, berrys,etc. They were always gathered, dried, and stashed away for the future, and resorted to often. The only medicines I can recall being over the counter varieties were those delivered by local sales reps for The Watkins Company or Raleigh Companies. These were peddled from household to household and were eagerly sought after by folks along the creek. Most of these were lotions, salves, and ointments of a rub on nature. There were no pill cabinets, most healing was done from applying some concoction to the exterior of the body. I remember the Raleigh man on Buffalo was actually not a man, but the beautiful daughter of Dan Robinson, and she rode a beautiful, big white horse up and down the creek and hollow delivering her products. I was just a tiny boy and thought her old, but she ended up marrying our Highland school teacher when I was in the second grade. So, she was probably just in her late teens. I still like and buy Raleigh products when I run across them and swear by the white liniment for mild arthritis.

There were other methods of non-traditional healing indulged in from time to time. These had been passed down for years and probably came to America with the early immigrants. Certain people had certain gifts and could cure some of the minor little day to day health issues. Thrash was a common ailment among babies and small children. There was a man on the creek who was said to be the son of a seventh son, and some people trusted and called on him in times of trouble, especially for the thrash. I recall him being a rather dirty, unkempt, slovenly individual, with tobacco stained teeth. Since my description of him is not very flattering I will forego his name. The method he used to cure the trash of an infant or a child was a simple one. He merely blew his breath in their mouth a few times. My mother availed herself of his services in treating her children this way a few times, and I was one of those lucky little fellows who benefited from the curing abilities of this man. I don't recall exactly how I felt about this guy blowing in my mouth, but I was probably too young to recoil in horror. Whatever my thoughts though, this guy was in demand from time to time and the children were healed. They also healed quickly, most by the next day.

There were other simple ills such as worms, warts, colds etc. I had several warts form on my hands once, and this same fellow came by. Mom demanded I show him my hands and she asked him if he could remove them. He looked at my hands, told her to bring him a short length of black sewing thread, then he proceeded to tie a knot in that thread, a knot for each wart. Then, he gave it to me and pointed to a place on the ground just under the eve of the house. He told me to scratch out a small hole and bury that thread there. It had to be where the rain waters coming off the roof would fall on the buried thread. Within a week or two my warts were gone. Now a child has faith, and maybe that is where the cure came from. Regardless, a lot of these old superstitions worked and it's not my intent to agree or disagree. I only know what I saw growing up.

There were other medical means of dealing with children's health. I remember that fowl tasting castor oil that was poured down your throat at the first sign of a stomach complaint. I'd usually withdraw my complaint and get better the minute I saw my mother head my way with a spoon and bottle of that terrible stuff. It was not uncommon for head lice to make an appearance in the community, and if one caught them, his hair was instantly scrubbed and washed with coal oil, or what now is mostly known as kerosene. Of course, there were some of the hardcore illnesses that I can't recall any home remedies for, but then I don't really recall them happening too often either. Complications such as the mumps, measles, etc, were usually healed by time, and the body itself. Of course, the big sicknesses were TB, Polio, and Smallpox. However, by the time my generation was reaching school age, vaccines had been developed to ward off these monsters. County Health nurses were making the rounds, some in vehicles, others on horseback, visiting all the little one room schools and lining the kids up for vaccination. I remember the ones coming to my school always brought a bushel of pears, or peaches. With the injection, you would be handed one of those ripe and delicious treats. It certainly helped take the edge off what one perceived as a painful experience. At least it made you forget quickly. These vaccines came in time to save thousands in my generation. Thankfully, both my oldest brothers survived polio, and suffered no crippling effects from it, but that was rarely the case in those days. Thanks to the injections I did not have to confront it.

Even though there was sickness in those days, I recall it being small compared to the maladies that people of today suffer. It did exist, but today, the biggest business in the world is that of treating the ill, and they are around, and among almost every family. The deaths I recall of my young years were mostly those of the elderly. Today, rampart cancers and other ills are consuming the population at an alarming rate. Death no longer waits for one's life to run its course. I recall a much more healthy, vibrant, society. This relates to mental as well as physical illness. I don't know if it was the home raised diet, the hard work, the rugged and rough outdoor life, or a combination of all the above. Or could the fault be with today? The constant doctoring and medicating from the cradle to the grave. The massive chemical poisons in our food supplies. The ever filling of our run off water supplies by round up and other herbicides and insecticides, but that's another field all by itself.

Since I'm under the weather I'm mostly dwelling on sickness I know today and

yesterday. The pundits can figure the rest, but I throw it in as just a thought. Now back

to another episode of an infected tooth and another round of Ibuprofen with some

penicillin vk..OUCH

The New Ground

Recently, I took a strenuous walk over a small portion of what once was referred to, as New Ground. It was strenuous activity, mainly because of my advance age. True, it's a steep, rocky area of hillside, but a few years back it would have been only a moderate trek at best. I went there following after old memories. This is important to mountain folks as they advance in age. Most all of them long to go back to the place of their childhood. Many do, others just come back briefly for short periods of time. It's a pattern pretty much regulated to those who grew up in the Appalachian Chain. It's something about those hills that seems to torment one's souls in their later years. Many acts on it, others dream about it, and many passes away in faraway States and Cities longing for, but never fulfilling, that desire.

It's my experience that this phenomenon is mostly related to Mountain folks. I suppose it's just to seek a connection to the wonderful childhood memories that we once knew. That was what I was looking for, and I always find it when I go searching. This old forested hillside did not let me down. It now is covered with Poplar, Hickory, Oak and the many other native species that abound in Appalachia. It appears now, as it did the first time I recall seeing it.

Then there came a time when my father decided we had pretty much worn out all the good gardening and corn growing ground. That happened in those days as there was little, if any, good fertilizer to buy. Even if there had been, money would not have been available to buy such stuff. The manure from the livestock was the only fertilizer we knew, and there was not enough of that to supply the nutrients to all those little fields of corn and crops that provided a living on a substance farm. The hill people improvised, and would go up and fall the timber on a hillside, saw or chop it up, then drag it away to the side, uncovering a large area of fertile black soil which would provide crop nutrients for several years to come. Then, as that area became poor soil, they would go elsewhere and do the process all over again.

I was not old enough to be much help, but Dad would always take me along and I'd play while he wielded an ax and cut those large trees. It was hard back breaking work, and I'd observe this man as the sweat poured from his brow. After clearing a little area at a time, he would follow through by bringing the faithful old mule, and pulling all those limbs and tree trunks off to the side. A little at a time and in a few weeks, a large area would be clean, with the exception of the stumps. It would be a long time before those stumps would be removed, but that did not hinder the planting of the corn. The old mule would make a feeble attempt at pulling the plow but it was mostly like chicken scratching. That did not stop the planting though, the soil was scratched up enough to get seed in the ground, and the corn would grow tall and green in the new earth. Many rocks would be carried out and heaped in piles. Those rock piles made my memories real. They are still there, just like the day he piled them. If not for those rocks and my memory, one would never know that corn had ever grown here.

The huge forest had reclaimed its own and blighted out any evidence that man had tread and worked here. I saw a pile that had one big rock on top and was tempted to set on it but knew too well it was snake time and any mountain boy knows all too well that rock piles are a haven for poisonous snakes, so I declined and settled for an old fallen tree to rest on instead. I thought a lot as I sat here. I thought about how labor intensive the work was for those old timers. I also thought about the people of today, and how so many of them don't have the concept of what real labor and work is. I also figured, if there is ever any societal breakdown, they would most all be short lived as they would have no idea on how to survive. I also thought about the phrase "White Privilege." No such a thing existed in the Mountains. There was no privilege for anyone. Black, White, Red or even Green should there have been such a color. They labored and broke down fairly young just feeding their families without handouts.

I observed a little flat area that I wasn't sure of, but thought it was the spot I played with my pet groundhog while dad worked. That groundhog was one of the best pets I ever had. Even in those woods he would stick by me and never once tried to wander off. I tried to remember what became of him but could not. I suppose like other wild pets I had as a youth, he got older and began to wander off. They would come back for a while, but their absence times would grow longer and longer until one day, they would be gone forever. I have never known if they went back to their wild nature or if they simply fell prey to some predator because of their tameness. I know now that my taming them was not in their best interest. I have to say though, that a groundhog makes one of the best pets a young child can have, and mine, whose name I can't recall, always stood patiently waiting for me to lift him to my shoulder. It was a place he loved to ride and nibble at my ears.

Then I remembered the rattlesnake. We had been around that stump several times when I saw my father go get the hoe, and come back chopping at something near that trunk. Even though he tried to show me before he killed the snake, I could not see it until he drug it out in the open. A rattlesnake's ability to blend in with its surroundings is amazing. I recall that I thought that snake was one of the most beautiful creatures I had ever seen, and felt remorse that it was dead. I still think a rattlesnake is a beautiful creature but certainly don't want to share my habitat with one. The old blacksnake that lived in our barn was a fascination to me, and in the spring when he shed his skin I could think of no creature more beautiful. So, it was only natural that I would find that rattlesnake attractive. Knowing that something that beautiful that could be so deadly made it even more entertaining.

I walked away from a place that once brought me great joy. A place that once helped feed our family with nothing asked in return except a little hard work. My thoughts were a little sad, but there was a mixture of happiness too. There was the knowledge that at one time, I had been part of this new ground, and it appeared it was richer, by far, from where we had left off.

The Haunted House

A few days back I took a walk around our original old home place. I refer to it as the original, because it's where I was born, and my first memories took hold. It's also the spot that for whatever reason, holds my most cherished childhood memories. It was a misty, dreary, damp December day. The sort of day where one's mood is very easily prone to sadness. A sadness of memories that were once happy and cheerful. I eased my way up the hillside a short distance so I could look down at the little cleared area where the old house and outbuildings once sat.

Though they have been gone for years, I could still visualize them in my mind. I had stared down from this vantage point many times as a child and those images are very well formed deep in the vaults of my brain. There was a mist over the little garden area on this day, and up and along the hillsides, other little misty spirals were creeping up from the earth and disappearing into the somber darkness of the sky.

For whatever reason my eyes focused on an area where the county road now runs. That road goes across the end of what, at one time, was our most productive garden spot. Whenever my father was gardening, I was always by his side, having a good time playing in the cool mountain soil. There is something about the newness of fresh plowed earth that a young child finds enticing. At least that was the way with us young children on Buffalo Creek. If we could not get our hands dirty, then our day of play had not been a success.

Many thoughts went through my mind looking down that hill. Then again, my eyes focused on the area of the little county road. I suppose it was the dreariness of the day that brought it to mind, but I recalled playing there one day while my dad made sweet potato hills. During my play, near the end of the garden and where the road is now located, he stopped for a while, and resting on his hoe, pointed to a little area off behind a briar patch. He informed me that the body of a little baby was buried there, and that he never plowed that area for that reason. This was something he should have never told me, as a young child's curiosity is forever searching for the unusual.

So, it was that in the late evening hours, while most of the family was on the front porch, I kept badgering him to tell me about the baby. Finally, giving in, he related the story that is one of the most fantastic tales I ever heard him tell. I have carried it all my life and not a year goes by that I don't think of it several times. At the time he said, my Mothers Grandma and Grandpa Burns lived in the house and they always told him the house was haunted.

There were days and nights that the frightening crying of a baby would occur. Even in daylight hours when they were outside, the stillness of a Buffalo day would be shattered by that piercing cry. Many of a trip back into the house occurred in an effort to locate the source. At nights they were often awakened, but when they'd arise from the bed to search it out, silence would return. Later, he and my mother, and my two oldest brothers (whom were just more or less babies themselves), moved into the house with my Mother's Grandparents. They were old and Dad and Mom were needed, so it was a good deal for all concerned.

The Grandparents lived only a few short years or less and my parents continued living there for several years after. I was raised to a great big boy there but never did know, or remember, my Great Grandparents. Sometimes weeks would go by, occasionally a few months, but the crying baby always returned to haunt my dad.

Then, one day he decided to do some work on the old place. The old house had a double fireplace that fronted into each of the two main rooms. However, each of those rooms had to be accessed by outside entry. To go from one to the other, you had to exit to the front porch, then go through another door to the other room. On each side of the fireplace were little built in closets. My father's idea, was to remove one of those closets, and create a means of passage to one room to the other, without the need to exit outdoors. Thus, it was this little project that brought forth and solved the mystery of the crying baby. When he tore those boards away and exposed one side of the old stone chimney, there just above his head, laying on one of the chimney step rocks, was a bundle of rags. His first thought was an old rats nest. He reached up to investigate further, and could feel something besides just cloth. Encompassing the entire bundle of rotted rags, he gently lifted it and brought it out into more light, and there in the middle, was the perfect figure of a newborn baby. Skin like leather, but completely preserved. There next to the heat of the chimney rocks, it had mummified.

Those were different times, and people never gave second thought to things that had happened in the past, and they never, ever thought of calling any kind of law. They were a world unto themselves, and the only thing they considered in this case, was to give the baby a proper burial. I know a crying baby or a haunt story is pretty much too far-fetched for most to believe, but there is no doubt in my mind on the dead baby, even though there were no officials called, the finding and burial of the baby was not unknown by some others on the creek.

I would be far up in mid-life before I really took an interest in this story, and found a few old-time family who verified the baby part. Outside my parents, I have never been able to verify the crying part, but not many years back It was confided to me who the mother of the baby was, and she would have been living there in the right time frame. She is long departed, but still has many grandkids along with other family, so I won't be naming any names. Anyway, she departed the area in the fifties, and most of her descendants were raised elsewhere.

My father was a mountain man, they believed in ghosts, but they also believed in improving any story they told. The crying part, or the haunting part, could very well have been added to make a more impressive story, plus the telling of supernatural tales in the late evening hours was a mountain tradition. Few folks on Buffalo, or Owsley County for that matter, especially those of his generation, would deny that ghosts existed. As for how callous they regarded the finding of a body or bringing outsiders in, I can recall myself when the county-built part of the new road up Buffalo and rooted up a body just above Mrs. Betty Gabbards place. The human bones were beside the road for weeks, and the skull was played with along the creek.

So, it was, that I found myself looking through the mist and down the hill side. As I looked I thought about a baby, wrapped in some old rags, and later probably plowed away by a county road grader. I wondered about the Mother. She had many children later, so was she just a young unmarried girl, scared, frightened, and delivered a stillborn? Did anyone else know? Was there anyone she could have confided in? Was it the times? Was she deathly scared and maybe killed or smothered the baby herself?

The child would have been a bastard child in those days, and both she and it would have been sort of outcasts.

She was related to me, so I thought about the baby. Could it have really been a spiritual cry for help to remove itself from its lonely confinement and returned to the earth? I like to think my dad added to the story, but I have been around enough in those dark and brooding hills, that I really don't question. As I have said before, there are many mysteries there...

Nicknames

Tootle socks, Ditze, Beardy, Little Hack, Tubby, Big Ears, Stick, Skeets, Hi-Pockets, Big Chicken, Little Chicken, Rubber Legs, Dab Eyes, Sonny Boy, Keg head, Syrup Head, Snake, Jinks, Runt, City Boy. All just a string of weird words that are stretched through my mind like knots on a string. Of what significance are they? Really little, except dwelling on my remembrances of coming of age in the small community of Oneida, they come to my mind fondly.

These were some of the characters I recall. None of those words were real names, but were what we commonly called nicknames. They were names affectionately attached to individuals by family and friends. Once those names were attached to a person, it never went away, and followed that individual to his grave. The real name of that person would seldom ever be spoken again. Most boys, at some point in their young lives, would acquire such a distinguished honor. I believe there were a higher percentage of nicknames around Oneida than any other place I ever resided.

The name was often given due to some physical characteristic, or some personality trait, or some activity that the person so named was involved with. I was never awarded a nickname so I must have been a pretty common individual in the area. I recall my brother listening to some persons speaking of another, and the name they kept saying was Cat's Ass. His curiosity got the best of him, and he asked, " why do you call him Cat's Ass?" Which returned an appropriate response from those individuals, "Hell, ain't you never looked at his face?"

So, it was with nicknames. Maybe I was fortunate not to have had one, because in some cases, it was not always flattering. The few I listed were some I recall, but in no way is the list comprehensive. The vast ocean of days between the fifties and sixties, and today has erased many nicknames from my mind.

What ever happened to that great tradition of passing out nicknames? Has the easy flow of humor and banter been wiped out by the tense world of political correctness that we have had forced upon us? Would it not be nice to see "Short Legs" again, and warmly say hello, and in uttering that nickname get a big, affectionate grin in return? They were just nicknames, but their loss is a sign of things that go deeper than that. We are losing a lot in society, and the infamous nicknames are just a small portion.

Thoughts on James Barrett

James Barrett and I go back many years. We were both old Clay County Kentucky boys and traveled a big portion of life's highway as friends. It was sometime in the eighties when James and I, along with a fellow by the name of Eddie Johnson, started us up a small business. We all had interest elsewhere, but was hoping to build something that we could tinker with and maybe even make a living from. It was an automotive related enterprise and we eagerly took it on.

We bought a couple of vans, some pressure washing equipment, and launched our new adventure. We located it near downtown Lexington and appropriately named it Fleet Automotive care. We hired a few employees and a young UK student to do phone solicitations. Everything we did was mobile, and included minor mechanics, oil and grease, pressure washing, auto detailing, and things of that nature. I think we were moderately surprised to find that in just a couple of months the business was paying its way, which is unusual for a new venture. Even then it was hard to find good, responsible employees. Not as much as today, but nonetheless, it was a big problem.

Folks liked the idea of us coming to their place of business, and it freed them up from worrying about such little items as oil changes, brake jobs, or just having their vehicle serviced and detailed in their driveway. We soon had six employees on the road and prospects were looking good. We had numerous clients and many were individuals who could afford and liked the idea of being pandered to without leaving home.

Some of the fleets I recall were auto dealers. Others were bigger companies such as Coca Cola, Zee Medical, and Oliver Trucking out of Winchester. I had no doubts then, nor now, that if we could have committed ourselves full time, instead of having to depend on employees, that the concept would have went over well.

One day I had to let a couple of guys go because they were caught drinking on the job. This created a problem and we were desperately in need of a couple of employees quickly. Just like a gift from heaven this guy walked in off the street and filled my head with all kinds of qualifications. He sounded perfect, but in a bind, we had no time to do any kind of check on him and hired him on the spot. A day or so later I gave him a key to the shop. A few days later one of the employees arrived early and called me, informing me that we had been robbed. I hurried to Lexington and walked into a shop stripped of everything that one could haul away. Nothing of value was left. We filled out the required police report and held a meeting between us three owners. It was then decided that since we had no responsible people on hand to look after our interest, we should start calling our clients and inform them we were suspending business operations for the time.

Even though the business was doing well and paying the employees, it had not reached the point that it would support us. The idea of floating a loan was not something we relished, so we voted to call it quits. A few weeks later, one of our vans was recovered in the medium of I-65 far up in Indiana, minus its cargo of any valuables that had been hauled away. I would run into Eddie Johnson only a few times after this. Then, not too long after, I stopped in his place of business in Lexington and asked for him. The secretary gave me a strange look, then informed me he had died over a month ago.

However, James and I remained friends for many years. The last several years he owned and operated a little S&T hardware store in McKee. On my travels I always stopped by and he and I would talk of olden times. We always laughed about us hiring an outlaw off the street and giving him a key to our chicken house. James, like me, found humor in most things, and as the years went on, the robbery became more amusing.

Several months back he called, asking me to come down to McKee to talk. I, of course went, as I take the request of any good friend serious. It seemed he had decided to run for State Representative and knowing I had managed a few campaigns before, wanted to know if I would go with him on this. I did not relish taking on any more politics at the time, but knowing he would be a formidable candidate, and it being a friend's request, I could not say no. I also knew that seat was winnable by him, because I knew James would do like he did everything else. He would put his whole heart into the endeavor.

We met a few times, discussing and planning. Then, just when it became time to think about that final step of filing, he informed me he had just found out he had cancer. His sickness became worse, and we decided it would be in the best interest of his health to forgo our plans for the time being. James, being the ever optimistic, said he would go the next time around after the Chemo and operations had healed his body.

I tried to visit him regularly after that, and I watched as week after week he kept digressing. During the last months I could not believe the difference in him from visits to visits. He went down so fast I was stunned, but he always had that warm smile and greeting. I went to see him the last time in Richmond Hospice a day or so ago. I found a man on his deathbed and wrecked with pain. Obviously, the strongest pain meds they had was not strong enough to bring him total peace. I don't know if he knew I was there or not. I became quite choked up, patted his now bony shoulder, and simply had to walk away.

I don't remember what I said to him, I was too grieved and shocked to see what this horrible thing of cancer had done to him. It was the first time in my life I'd ever seen James Barrett without that great big wonderful smile. His lips moved, I could not make out the words he tried to form, but his wife, setting by his bedside said those words were "I Love You." I sure hope so, because the feeling is certainly mutual old Pal. You were loved by not only me, but by every one that knew you. Your New business venture is now with God, and their good friend, success is guaranteed. You left this earth approximately eight hours after my visit, and I know you no longer suffer as mortals do. RIP JP

The Killing of Sill Collins – By Michael Dean

I believe it was about 1971 or 1972 when Sill Collins was killed by Raleigh Hensley, aka Raleigh Ho-babe. I'm not sure but I believe I was 16 years old when it happened. I think I was also 16 at the time of the trial. I suppose Oneida was a rough place back then. I witnessed several shootings growing up there as a teenager. Only two of those resulted in anyone being shot. One was the incident where Sill Collins was killed and Roger Campbell shot. The other was a couple of years after that. In the last one, the victim survived.

In any event, my recollection is as follows. I was with Roger Campbell, Sill Collins, Larry Burns, and David Baker that day. They were all older than me. I believe Roger was 24 and Sill was 19. We were all in a car together. Even though I was quite young, everybody had been drinking beer. I must not have drunk very much because, although, I can't remember details now, over 40 years later, I was very aware of everything that went on at the time. Nor do I remember what time of year it was. We were in Roger's car.

In any event we all stopped at Fannie Arnett's Restaurant across the old bridge in Oneida. I do remember it was dark at the time. At first, we were all in the Restaurant. I don't remember anyone else other than Fannie being there. I remember that Sill and maybe the rest of us ordered some hot dogs. For some reason, four of us walked outside on to the porch. It was a narrow concrete porch that ran across the front of the building, about 5 feet wide. We were all lined up standing on the porch except for Sill, who was still inside.

A car pulled up and it was Raleigh Hensley. He got out of the car with two guns. He had a pistol in one hand and a rifle in the other. At the time Raleigh was like an old man to me but he was probably in his fifties. He walked towards us on the porch. Roger Campbell said "what are you gonna do with them guns Raleigh?" I remember Raleigh saying "I will show you By God," and Raleigh shot Roger. As I remember, Roger was closest to the door, which was located in the center of the building. The rest of us were lined up on the left of the door if you are facing the building. As soon as Raleigh started shooting, Roger ran past the rest of us on the narrow porch to get away. None of us were armed. By then, I remember that Raleigh was up on, or at the edge of the porch, firing at Roger as he ran past us.

About that time, Sill Collins came out the door and said something like "what's goin' on?" Raleigh was right there in front of Sill when he came through the door. Raleigh turned to Sill and shot him point blank, it's hard to remember but seems like Raleigh shot him again after he fell down. I do distinctly remember Sill saying after being shot the first time as he went down, "Lord have mercy on me!" Sill probably died immediately. After Raleigh shot Sill, the rest of us took off running to get away from him. David Baker, Larry Burns and me ran across the bridge. They went first and I followed them. Roger had run around the building. I believe Roger has been shot twice, once in the arm and maybe another in the back.

As we were running across the bridge, I remember hearing more gunshots. After the shooting, Roger's two sisters, a friend of theirs, and a couple of kids drove up. As I recall from talking to some of them later, and based on what they said at the trial, they had seen Sill's body on the ground and saw Roger's car in the parking lot. They were concerned and stopped to see what happened. Some of them got out of the car and asked Raleigh, who was the only person standing there, where their brother was. Raleigh cursed and told them something to the effect that he had killed Roger and would kill them too if they didn't get in the car and get up the road. As they were trying to leave, Raleigh shot at least twice into the car. Somehow miraculously, the bullets never hit anyone. I looked at the car later and saw the bullet holes in the back seat.

I walked home that night. I later testified at Raleigh's trial. Raleigh testified that Roger and Sill tried to rob him and that he was just defending himself. It was clearly a lie. I don't know if the jury believed him, but he received a 15-year sentence for the murder.

Murder In Oneida

I suppose by now it's pretty well understood that I spent a lot of my childhood on Upper Buffalo Creek in Owsley County, Kentucky. It was a youth spent in Idealism and pursuit of childish adventure. There were a few bad things that happened on Buffalo during that time period, but little of those things concerned my family, so it was of little notice or consequence to me as a child. Those bad things were distant from family and so I, as a child, payed little attention. It would be sometime down the road of time that we would relocate to the Oneida area of Clay County, and there I would grow into and through my adolescent years. For me to tell about the Oneida of that place and time would require a lot of material.

I have intended to write about those years, but have barely scratched the surface. One of the reasons I have not is due to the fact that most people would find it hard to believe the wildness and craziness of that place during those post war years and beyond. The exception would be those few folks that are still around and grew up there when I did. Many are no longer around, but the ones that are can relate to how it really was and know that I would not be stretching the truth with what I share.

Oneida was much like a staged play, with a cast of strange and motley characters, who possessed personalities of a kind that I have seldom encountered since. So, it is that those who were young in the fifties and sixties would well remember the shenanigans and wild west atmosphere that prevailed.

In my young adult life, I rambled and spent time on the streets of some of America's major cities. The South Side of Chicago comes to mind, but for sheer lawlessness and high-spirited disruptions, Oneida would in that day run a close second. Granted it was not as violent, and it was mostly activities of a non-violent nature and consisted of young folks just generally raising hell for the fun of it. In town drag racing late at night was commonplace, and on a pretty weekend the races could occur anytime during daylight as well. Firing of guns during the night and blasting out a street light or two was not an uncommon event. Drinking and brawling was known to occur pretty regularly, but most of those wild youths I recall would later settle down and become stable citizens and raise families who are still in the area today.

What I wonder about now is the older folks, the ones living in town with families. How did they tolerate such happenings, and how did they sleep through it? Many of them would have to have been early risers as they had jobs, positions, and business to attend to. I guess over time they built an immunity and slept through it all. There was little law after hours, and often none at all.

As I said, it was mostly harmless fun and recklessness, and even the brawlers would be seen together the next day, friends all over again. However, in this wild town atmosphere violence would sometimes raise its ugly head. I can recall several instances of that happening.

Last night, sitting on the porch and reminiscing with my brother Michael, we got to rehashing one of those violent episodes. It was an event that came close to costing my younger brothers life. The year was 1971 or maybe 72. Neither of us could recall the exact time frame. What little I knew of the event was all second hand, but his knowledge was that of an eye witness. It gave me a good chance to get the real story and for memory sake I encouraged him to write it all down.

On that day he had fell into the company of Roger Campbell, and Sill Collins. In the gang also was Larry Burns and David Baker. As young folks so often did, they acquired a few beers and had been riding around sipping and enjoying their beverages. When darkness came they found themselves at Arnett's restaurant, which sat near the end of the bridge across the river from Oneida. It was a popular hangout at the time. Unknown to Mike, Larry Burns and David Baker, Roger and Sill had previously had some sort of altercation with one Raleigh Hensley, locally known as little Rall, or Raleigh Ho-Babe. It was a lack of knowledge that nearly cost them their lives. They had all indulged in a few hot dogs and Roger, Mike, David, and Larry stepped out on the porch.

They were all lined up along the porch when Raleigh Hensley pulled into the parking lot. He exited his car and came towards the porch carrying a pistol in one hand and a rifle in the other. As he reached the porch Roger Campbell asked, "Where you going with the guns Raleigh?" The quick verbal response was, "By God I'll show you," at which time he shot Roger point blank. Roger was not downed by the bullet but bolted around the corner as Raleigh continued to fire at him. At that moment Sill Collins had the misfortune to come out the door asking, "What's Going On out here?" Raleigh then shot him at point blank. By now Mike and the other two was running across the bridge in the darkness, and could hear shots continue to be fired. Rogers Campbell's sister, along with some kids pulled up, probably just a chance encounter, but they saw Sill's body and Roger's car in the lot, and yelled "Where is Roger?" The reply from Raleigh was, "I killed him and if you don't hit the road I'll do the same to you." They left the scene rapidly, but Raleigh, regardless, in a drunken rage fired at the car, putting two bullets in it as it roared away. He was now a crazed person totally out of control.

Amazingly, Raleigh only received fifteen years for the crimes, and I think he only stayed three or four of those years. Those years he served, he served as a trustee at the PeeWee Valley institute for women, near Lagrange. He had a room in the basement of that complex and tended to do the handiwork around the place. His time was served in a very easy manner. The reason I know this is that in 1974, or thereabouts, I was sent to work for a couple of weeks at this institution. It was just for a couple of weeks and a temporary assignment, and then I was to return to Frankfort. I was working the security gate mostly. On about my third day, the buzzer went off from inside the yard, which meant someone was asking to enter. The intercom informed me it was the janitor. I pressed the button to allow entrance. I don't know who was surprised more, myself, or Little Raleigh, because that is who came through that door. For the next several days Raleigh would come by for brief periods, and I would always grant him admittance.

I never brought the crime up, nor did he. If the higher ups knew the connections between us, one of us would have been transferred and it mostly likely would have been him. The thing I remember about the Raleigh of my Oneida years is that he was a pretty meek and humble person. Easy going, easy to talk to. It was when he would start drinking that he would become a bad man, totally crazed in most cases, and it took very little drink to get him to that point.

After a couple of weeks, I left and went back to Frankfort. My last day I said goodbye to little Rall and a few others. I don't recall ever seeing him again. It was not too long after that, he himself got released. I don't think he lived long after being paroled out. Would he have killed those other guys, without reason? Yes, I don't think there is any doubt. The proof of him shooting at a woman and some kids in a car is enough to convince me of that.

Thankfully, my brother escaped from this man's rage and lived to enjoy a successful life. He would later attend UK, become an engineer, work for several major coal companies, then decide that was not for him. Later he would attend the University of Virginia Law School and practice Law for many years. He presently serves as Circuit Judge for Lee, Owsley, and Estill Counties. I have tried to record this the best I can from the info he provided, but his brief sketch of the event is much more simple and explainable. It is with that thought in mind that within the next few days I will share his eyewitness account of this violent crime. As for Roger Campbell, Larry Burns, and David Baker, the last I knew they were still living.

Great Grandpa Ezekial Dean, The War Hero...

Growing up I heard a lot of stories about My Great Grandpa. Those stories came from old folks, whom could recall him when they were children. Dewey Fox comes to mind, as he was always ready to tell Zeke stories. He told me that when he was a child, Old Man Zeke was a fearsome looking individual. He mentioned that all the children his age were afraid of the old man. Dewey said Zeke most always wore black, and walked the creek beds with a long walking stick that contained a spike protruding from the end. Of course, he said in later life he realized that spike was for walking on the ice of the creek.

One dark winter morning Dewey and some boys were walking up the creek. It was a cold, damp time, and a dense fog was hovering over the water. It was then that they noticed the figure of Zeke appearing out of that fog, and coming their way. They were a little uneasy but Dewey got up a little bravo and thought he'd show his pals he was not afraid. The boys with him took to the bank to give Zeke the creek, and to stay clear, but Dewey aimed right at his direction. He said the old fellow in those black clothes, and that waist long beard, coming out of the fog, looked like a true devil. He admitted he was scared, but said when he got alongside Zeke, he asked, "What you doing with that old spiked cane old man?" He said and before he had time to think, the old fellow rammed that cain towards him, and it stopped about eight inches from his face. "This, young man, is to kill biting dogs and smart assed little boys." Dewey said before one could blink an eye he was up on the bank with his buddies. "That old man was not to be trifled with," he said.

I have a big picture of Zeke on my wall, and I can see why some would fear him, especially the very young. Dewey told me other tales on this ancestor but to dwell on them, I'd never get around to the hero part. Others way back in time, who recalled him, said he was a very mean, grouchy individual. However, as often is the case, there is in his pension files several affidavits praising him as a hardworking, old mountain farmer, trying to eck a living out of three hundred acres of steep, poor hillside.

The fellow, now well up in age, had left his home and moved to the Teges area of Clay County, because his wife and adult children mistreated him so bad. The files do support the fact that he walked out, leaving the farm, the livestock, and the crops in the ground. Which version is true cannot be said for sure, as there was a legal battle going on whereby his wife was seeking to get fifty percent of his Civil War pension. So, both sides were bringing forth witness. That pension he drew amounted to $72.00 a month. Probably a pretty tidy amount back then, and well worth fighting for. I always heard that he drew a check for a wound he received, and naturally assumed it was in combat. I acquired copies of his applications, affidavits, etc. from my brother, Michael Dean.

The first thing I noticed was that CO "I" 14th Ky. Calvary did not see any combat for the period in which he claimed for his wound. A little more reading explained that he did, or at least supposedly received a gunshot wound to the back of his head, which gave him much back and neck problems in later years. Then, there on the pension claim form it all comes to light. CO- I of the 14th Ky. was taking a rest at

Boonesborough. They had dismounted beside the road near some rail fences. The horses were tied to the rail fence, and the guns leaned against the same. Ezekial, like any good Dean would have done, found himself in a horizontal position and lying in the shade. Somehow, something, or someone spooked the horses, some tore away from the fence and knocked several rifles over. One of those rifles was primed and cocked, and when it fell a horse stepped on it triggering the hammer. That shot grazed the back of his head and created a pretty bad wound.

Now, as to the truth of this, the file is full of affidavits as to my Great Grandfathers condition and suffering from said wound many years later. He also was granted the pension for the wound, and drew said pension until he died. Now why do I call him a hero? How many of your ancestors have had the distinction of being shot by a horse and getting a military pension for it? That goes far beyond cool, and verges on some type of great medal. I may have to apply to get the honors due him.

The Stray Dog

There's been a stray dog rambling the neighborhood. Actually, I should say a strange dog, as he seems healthy enough and his body weight looks good. Maybe a lost dog would be more accurate. There are lots of dogs in our neighborhood, and most are well known. You might say our street is sort of a safe haven, and most on the block own dogs. I watched the guy cross my yard this morning and got to thinking of dogs.

In general, I started thinking back to the dogs and other animals I had around me in my youth. Most animals I grew up with on Buffalo were beasts of burden, or animals for food. I don't recall a lot of pets per say, especially household pets. Sure, most households had a dog, but it was most often an outdoor dog, and it either had the ability to hunt, or some other trait to help earn its place as a member of the family. The dog lived outside, and his food consisted of what scraps were spared or left from the family's meals. Since most scraps, along with dishwater were regulated to be placed in the slop barrel, the dogs share was often very meager. I simply can't recall house dogs. I am sure they must have been some on the creek, but they somehow escaped my memories.

I myself cannot recall having a pet dog as a child. The few we had were hunters, and helped father supply the game that was a good portion of our diet. The one pet I can recall was a groundhog whom I kept in an outdoor cage, and carried it to the fields when Dad would be working there. That groundhog and I would frolic and play in that cool, soft earth for hours. Today, I see few groundhogs, they are nowhere as abundant as they once were, but when I see a young one my mind fleetingly thinks of capturing it for one of my grand babies. But in the end good judgement prevails.

Us kids also had the misfortune to make a pet out of one of our young meat hogs, which would follow us around the old place and we enjoyed its presence immensely. That hog would disappear one cold December day while we were at school. I suppose she was added to the meat supply in our smokehouse. The hard and seasoned mountain folks, hard pressed to keep a large family fed, knew animals as a means to do just that. They could not let the luxury of having a pet interfere, and they allowed themselves little kindness or emotional attachment to the livestock, dogs, horses etc. Stray dogs, like predator birds, and animals were also not tolerated. Anything as a threat to their chickens, or livestock was summarily executed. Additionally, well up into the 1950's rabies was a real threat, and an outbreak here and there was not uncommon. Such an outbreak could spread quickly in a county and it brought great fear with it.

Once while working in Letcher County, I encountered an old man of eighty some years, who loved to remember and talk of his childhood. The conversation drifted around to how many people back in that time period was cruel to animals.

As a young boy, he had briefly worked for some of the big timber interest, and said they lost mules daily from broken legs. They were then shot. The company kept lots of extra mules to throw into the work when the daily losses occurred.

However, my favorite story was one that took place in the early part of the century. He said he was just a young child when a vicious outbreak of rabies swept the county. It got so bad that the Courts dispatched the Sheriff to kill off the dog population in the county. Even home pets were to be eradicated. People were panicking as the virus was cropping up everywhere. Sitting on his porch he saw far down the mountain, a group of armed men headed up the foot path to his mountain home. Having heard a few days prior to the counties decision, he knew instantly what they were there for. Running around back he leashed his little dog and headed to the mountaintop. There he penned her under a rock shelter and for the next several days packed her food. As a result, his little dog survived to die of old age.

In a few weeks the fear and rabies had subsided and he was able to turn her loose and enjoy his dog again. I would have discounted his story except as a reader of early history I have actually encountered the same situation from the early part of the 19th century where by the Sheriff did eradicate the entire dog population in efforts to bring rabies outbreaks under control. I remember an old stray dog popping up near our home when I was a lad. He would not come close to the house but would keep his distance, which showed him to be wise indeed, and also showed that he had probably been shot at from some other houses. I'd get a piece of cornbread from the oven warmer and throw it a great distance. He would then take it with great delight. I had begun to refer to him as "Old Ruff", as he was a pretty tough looking breed. I did not see him for a week or so, and then one day playing in a hole of water near our house, I saw him coming up the road. The road ran mainly in the creek but it cut sharply up the bank and went around the hole of water, then went back into the creek. I yelled at him but strangely he never looked my way, and as he got beyond and farther up the road I noticed he would wobble and almost fall. He's sick, I was thinking.

A few days later I heard a group of men further up the creek saying they had killed and disposed of a mad dog by burning its body. I knew instantly, it had to be old Ruff. Curiosity got the best of me, so I walked the few miles to the rock bar where the disposal had taken place. There was a pile of ashes, a few charred ends of sticks and small logs. It had been a hot fire and no evidence was left of the dog's body.

On that hot, sultry, August day, I was probably a mighty lucky kid that the old fellow did not have the ability left to see or even notice me when I called to him. That is the only time I can recall encountering a mad dog in my youth, but on various hunting trips I have encountered a few possums and raccoons during daylight hours that displayed all the symptoms. From my childhood, I learned that if you encounter nocturnal animals during daylight hours, make a wide detour. Especially in the hot days of Summer.

Remembering John Baker

Overcast and cold today. The winds seem to be primarily from the South West, and carries with them lite snow squalls. It's the 9th day of December, 2017. I have mostly stayed shut in today, as I don't care to deal with this blustery weather. Besides, the Christmas shoppers are already out in force, and what running I had to do today, I accomplished in the early morning hours. I have watched a little TV, touched base on the computer, and as always read a lot.

I have had moments to think and recall scenes of years gone by. Those thoughts have pretty much dealt with my young days on Buffalo Creek, and the many folks I recall. I know not why, but dark days takes me backwards now and sometimes can bring a tinge of sadness. It's also the Holiday Season, and I have been down the Christmas paths so many times, I suppose I have developed an immunity to the craziness of this time of the year. Today's thoughts have been good though. They were good memories and I enjoyed traveling back to the fifties and observing some of the older boys that us young kids used to be around.

There were lots of young people on Buffalo at that time, and that generation was an active and happy crew. Most of those older teens I thought on today are gone, and the few that are left would range in age from the late seventies to early eighties. Thinking on those individuals, I am reminded that us young grade schoolers, of the same time period are following close on their heels. My brothers, Wayne and Albert, were part of that older crew. Wayne still lives, and resides in Florida. Albert has been gone several years now, and he lies at rest in a little scenic spot in Clay County, along with my Mom and Dad and many other family members.

I have also had John Baker on my mind. He was one of many children born to Chester and Cathrine Baker. Where you found Wayne, Albert, and the rest of that age group you would find John. I recall that bunch making Johnny Walkers, building wooden sleds when the winter snows fell, and even a few attempts at building rafts to float on the creek when the spring floods occurred. The best I remember, the rafting part was seldom successful, as Buffalo Creek was simply overgrown too much.

I remember John's father ran a little store at Highland. It sat on a bank above the road and there was a pretty steep incline on the road. John got together some saw mill lumber and built him a car. Things appear large to a young child, so I recall that contraption to be as big as an ordinary car. I am sure that was probably not the case, but I do know he had regular auto wheels on that thing. I was too young to be involved, but I did watch as he, and the older boys played. It was all running by gravity, except going uphill it required human power. They would pile on somewhere near the old store and ride it down the hill following the road. When the road leveled off at the bottom and their toy slowed and stopped, they would push it backwards to the top and repeat the scene all over. I don't recall or remember if they had breaking power or not. I was too young to be allowed a lift.

During those years John was a lot like his late Brother Al, and was forever seeking out critters and birds to capture. I remember two tame crows he had, and I don't recall them very fondly. I had scraped together a Nickel somewhere, and ambled my little bare-footed feet all the way to his father's store. There I purchased a candy bar and left, opening it up as I exited the store. I noticed on top of the building sat one of those crows. Not paying it any mind I went my way and was preparing for my first taste of that delicious treat, when all of a sudden, a moving shadow flashed, and before I had time to react that crow had scooped that treat from my hands and continued airborne to a large tree. I have to say I was devastated.

We would leave the creek not long after that and there was a period of a few years with no memories of John and the others. He would end up in the Army, my brother Wayne would go to the Navy, and the others in that crew would end up in other areas as well. I could spend a day talking about John but I just wanted to touch on some child hood memories.

Later in life Wanda and I married and moved to Frankfort. John Baker was living there at the time. I was now an adult, like him, and we became good friends. He loved to hunt, fish, and other outdoors activities. In addition, he, like me, had never forgotten Buffalo. Both of us, although at different times were always returning there to visit. Eventually, both of us would have cabins there, and in our later years visit often.

John and his wife Rose left Frankfort and bought a place in Rockcastle County. I think this was in the late seventies or early eighties. Over the years I visited there many times. It was mountain land and very private. They absolutely loved it. Like I said, he liked to hunt, and I'd venture to say he tried to eat every form of wildlife that existed in those days. I do know he liked possum and I don't think I ever visited that he didn't offer to get a possum out of the freezer. "We'll cook it up," He'd say. Fortunately, I was always able to put the possum meal off until some other time. I am not sure if he really had a possum, or was simply pulling my leg, but I really did not want to know. Knowing John though, I am betting he had more than one tucked in that freezer.

His wife Rose passed away about a year ago from a long-time battle with cancer. Wanda and I attended her visitation, and John appeared to be handling it well. I knew him though, as a person who did not like to be alone, and worried some about him. I made it a point to run down and visit several times, and could tell he was a very lonesome person without Rose. Ironically, just shortly after burying his wife, cancer, never being satisfied, attacked John as well. He went through all the treatments and medicines that could be given, and like many others, suffered through the side effects. Given what he thought was a clean bill of health, he was supposedly cancer free. It lasted a short time and then came back with a vengeance.

I made several trips to see this old Buffalo Friend and saw him go downhill fast. The last few weeks he has been home, attended and looked after by his family. I think this satisfied him. Home was a place he loved. I went to see him yesterday. I guess I should say I went to see his daughter, Sonda and the rest, as I knew well that John did not know anyone at this point.

I left from there yesterday about two or three in the afternoon and John Baker passed away at seven thirty last night. There are some memories left. Memories of hunting trips, fishing, camping, and just hanging out. John Baker lived his entire life as a good man and he is sure going to be missed.

The old folks from Buffalo that could tell you how it used to be are rapidly leaving the scene and my generation is right behind them. I am glad I knew John when I was a child. I am even more glad that I knew him as a friend when I became an adult. More than anything though, knowing John as I have over the years, I am glad that he got to leave this world at home, surrounded by family and friends. God bless them for being there.

Christmas Past

I don't get excited over Christmas anymore. I suppose that's because I have seen so many come and go. It is nothing more than a giant sale put on over a two-month period by the Nation's retailers. It's the economic heyday of the years. The period of the season when their profit margin for the entire year will either be a plus, or minus.

A poor sales season can be devastating. The stock market alone will rise and fall according to how many gullible people poured out their hard-earned dollars through December. Simply put, it's about cash. I don't have a problem with this, as it affects me little. I am not addicted to shopping, and if I want anything and can afford it, I prefer to buy it myself at my own time. How many little trinkets are around this house, stashed in the bottom of some drawer, or in a closet that was given to me by some beaming family member just knowing it was exactly what I needed. When in fact, I really needed nothing at all. However, I praised the gift because to do otherwise would be rude and uncaring. It was wonderful to know they had remembered me, but a simple Merry Christmas card would have been more than enough.

These entrapments were not always there. There was a time when Christmas had spirits. One knew it was special whether they received a gift or not. I lived in such a time. I often think back to those Christmas events on Buffalo. Most were poor as dirt, and gifts were far away from many of us. Being good or bad had nothing to do with it. Just the same, us kids would become excited a Month before. One could sense the Christmas Spirit in the air. Evergreens would be pulled off the hillsides, and placed in the corners of the little cottage. Many afternoons were spent sitting around the fireplace cutting angel figures, and paper chain links, all lovingly done in an artistic manner, to grace the boroughs of that little evergreen.

Then there were evenings in front of the old, kitchen stove where little children with needles would puncture the popped grains of corn, and spread it onto the string. After getting a strand long enough to encircle the tree several times, it was added as another part of the decoration. An old time Christmas tree is a beautiful work of art, and while an electrically lighted tree, with all its tinsel and manufactured ornaments is an awesome sight, it falls far short of the beauty of that old hand made, labor intensive, primitive tree of yesterday. One was a work of art, the other merely a manufactured creation of millions. The first built and put together with a labor of love, the latter put together in a factory, somewhere in China, most likely with immature labor, over worked, suffering from long hours, and just throwing it together with no thought except how many more must be done before he/she can get a brief respite from the toil, boredom, and exhaustion.

Our old trees were put together with family love. Not necessarily as a place to stash gifts, but to honor the Spirit of Christmas. In most cases they never saw a gift slipped beneath their branches. As a matter of fact, most Christmas activities were done to honor the Spirit of Christmas. Christmas Caroling was big, as groups of young from various churches would travel by truck bed or wagon, and take time to slow down in front of every house and belt out a Carol. Plays and activities were also performed, again most sponsored by churches.

In my case on Buffalo, our young people would for years to come, owe a large debt to the late Mr. and Mrs. Chester Ranck, who would lead us through so many Spirits of Christmas. It was through their ministry, that some of us were able to receive a few gifts during that special time. While we indulged in many festive activities, it was all about Christ, and there was none of us that did not feel the Christmas Spirit.

It was the happiest time of the year, and did not become so because of gifts or large expenditures. I always went to bed in the highest state of excitement knowing that it was Christmas eve and old St. Nicholas may very well make his appearance. He never failed to do so. I'd get up early, dash to the old fireplace, tear that stuffed stocking from the mantel and rush back to my warm bed. There on top of the covers I dump the contents. Some, hard candy, an apple, an orange, and in the very toe would be a handful of mixed nuts. The contents of that sock never changed over the years, and it was always received with joy and thanks. We could not have been happier.

Later in life I have thought about how my parents must have suffered through several hours of trying to keep awake until us excited kids would eventually fall asleep. Then, with much love they would tip toe in and stuff those socks with the pittance of what they could afford. Placed with much love, it was received by us kids in the same way. True it wasn't nothing by today's standards, but as little as the items were, they were things we only encountered a few times a year, which made them very special.

It was also Christmas, and we felt the love and spirit of the season. Even if there had not been a treat, the Spirit was out and about, and one could sense the air had a special feel to it, and the people and animals acted a certain way. One knew it was

Christmas then. I suppose I don't get too excited about Christmas anymore because much of that Spirit has been forsaken. It's about people anymore, economics, debt addiction.

It's as if we must buy family love, friend's love, or what we as individual's desire. It's not even about kids, grown-ups expect gifts now also. It's a mad, crazy season of traffic jams, road rage, crude bargain hunters, disrespectful customers, yelling and shoving, harassing poor salespeople whom have not the good fortune to be at home with family. I am not saying one should not buy a few gifts, but choose wisely, choose simply and for heaven's sake, choose one or two people whom you really think are in trouble and make a gift of help and assistance. And remember, Walmart and its competitors have absolutely nothing to do with the Season.

Whatever you do remember there is a Christmas Spirit, even though we are close to losing it. Try to relax and feel it. I have spent a few Christmas's alone on some trails, but laying and star gazing I felt, and knew it was Christmas. Don't ask me how, but Christmas, if one is totally alone, is still Christmas, and can bring a strong feeling of its Spirituality should one seek it. I find no more joy in that holy night than to hear the Carols, even they can pull on one's heart strings. As a matter of fact, sitting alone, or with family and loved ones, or with whomever, a good old-fashioned carol can awaken the Christmas Spirit better than about anything I know. You see, Christmas comes with a Spirit, and while you might make it through, and do what you suppose one should, if you don't feel a Spirit, then you are just stuck in another day.

I don't seek or want anything for Christmas. What I would want can't be given anyway. It would be a gift to be able to go back to a few Christmas's in the far past. To lay watching the shadow from the fire flicker around the hearth, and touch on those empty socks, and anticipating the morning when they will have magically been filled with goody's! To awaken to a day of Magic. A day of Spirit. A day different that all others in that Calendar year. It would be my wish to feel that again.

Christmas Comes once a year. I know not where it travels from to arrive, but the old plantation blacks in our early history thought we were wrong about Christmas coming. They adhered to the belief that Christmas never came, it always fell. It was with that in mind they would all gang up outside the little shanties a few moments before midnight and at exactly twelve-o-clock, they would hear the sound of the Christmas Spirits crashing to earth, and would let loose with much shouting and spiritual singing. Not one would say they did not hear Christmas fall.

Who knows? Maybe it comes, or maybe it falls, but the sound it makes gets less year after year. Maybe it's because the Christ is becoming less and less, and is being shut out more and more. One day, the Spirit of Christmas may not be heard at all.

Letters

Looking through one of our less used closets today, I pulled out an old shoe box and rummaged through it. Inside was a packet, held together by a now rotted rubber band. When I tried to pull the band off, it went into a dozen pieces. After separation, I discovered them to be old handwritten letters. They were not ancient, but old as it relates to my lifetime. The dates were the early seventies and the letters were from the time when Wanda and I were dating. It crossed my mind for a moment that we must never have thrown anything away. Opening and reading a couple of them, I thought them a tad silly. Then I remembered Wanda was just an adolescent, and I was just a young adult.

Thinking about the words and thoughts in those letters were exactly what one would expect from two young people far away from each other, and wishing they were together. Letters were always a big issue in my young life as I often found myself at a great distance from friends and family. It's hard for me to forget mail call. No matter where I rambled, I and everyone else, eagerly awaited those hand-written treasures. On the waters of Vietnam, or on an old merchant ship, mail was a looked to event, and when it arrived to be passed out, a sizable crowd always assembled.

However, mail was not just for those away and traveling. The arrival of letters to the folks at home was also eagerly looked forward to and many a young lady has sat looking from her window for the appearance of the mailman, with a fluttering heart hoping for some hand-written words of love from her betrothed. Her love who was working away, or serving in the military, or maybe living in a distant village. Parents looked forward to those hand-written letters from their children, containing the news of the birth of their grandchildren, or sickness, or success. It was a time of few phones, and a time of long distance expense if one could use a phone. The letter was the social media of the day, and I, like the rest of the country, loved the letters.

The vast majority of those crisp folded pages carried good news, but there were those few, that arrived at some point in time with heartbreaking, and sad news. Those were the family death notices, the dear John's, the announcement of illness in distant family. In all my young ramblings I can only recall a couple of letters that left me sad or heart broken. I can't even imagine being away from home today where it's a world of instant communication, instant texing, instant photos.

I imagine mail call now would be a small attended event to a young sailor or soldier. The handwritten personal letter has died, an inglorious death, with no mention, nor memorial of its passing. It won't be back. What, for two hundred years, moved our country's social connections left without a word of farewell, its demise was not even mentioned, never noticed, but in my heart the memories of so many happy moments, and thoughts shared on a piece of paper, bring back a lot of nostalgia. I slowly push the packet back into the shoe box. Its rested here, back in a corner shelf of this closet for many years. It's not my place to now throw it away. I hold the box a moment and think about how I looked forward to receiving or sending those letters those many years ago. I thought of the many lonesome miles I drove with my eyes searching eagerly for a pay phone. Pay phones. Well that is another thought for another time. RIP hand written letters.

Highway 150

After a long, dreary winter I get restless. The sun comes out and I start wanting to move. Today I left early and went rambling. The early part comes about because if I hang around the house a few hours, I become involved in one of those never-ending chores that an old house requires and thus my day is soon spent. Getting away before one of Wanda's to do list is mentioned becomes ever more important as I get older. Those hour-long chores take much longer now, and soon a day is washed away for eternity. I pacify her by agreeing to work three or four days a week at home. This, along with work at my other place, allows me two or three wandering days.

After a lot of winter shut in, I find getting out and about does wonders for my soul. Today, being in Mount Vernon, I headed west on highway 150 and drove to Standford. This is one of Kentucky's older roads, and at one time carried a lot of traffic. In those pre I-75 and I-64 days, it was also used heavily by trucks.

Now, the Interstates are much quicker, and to see a truck on old 150 is a rarity. There was a time many years back when this was a familiar highway to me. I lived in Frankfort at the time and would travel South on 127 to Danville and pick up 150 east. This would put me into Rockcastle County and connect me to my other work counties in East Kentucky.

The road I traveled today is a new road, and in no ways resembles the long, curvy route I drove in those days. It's a straight shoot all the way to Danville now. The old highway had a few little towns and villages, along with numerous businesses as it meandered its way east. As a matter of fact, I was completely lost on this new highway, and if not for a few signs pointing out Broadhead and Crab Orchard, I'd never have known they existed. I exited off at Broadhead and visited some longtime friends I had not seen in many years. It was good to see John Baker and his wife Rose. John is an old time Buffalo fellow, and also lived in Frankfort at one time when I did. If my memory is correct he has lived near this little community for about 35 years. I used to drop in and say hi in those long-gone years of the seventies and early eighties. They were a much younger couple then, and of course so was their visitor. There was no end to conversations about years gone by, but I only stayed about an hour, as Rose has suffered for a long time from cancer and still does. It was my wish not to wear her down, so it was a brief stop. Regardless, an enjoyable one.

Soon I was back on the road and was mildly surprised how quick one can reach Stanford from Mt. Vernon now. However, I'd liked to have traveled the old road, but it was blocked off in sections when the new one was completed. I did enjoy the long straight drive though, the weather was perfect, the natural spring beauty bounded on both sides, and traffic was virtually nonexistent. Thus, I had the privilege to observe and sight see as I drove. One thought crossed my mind concerning the traffic, there were so few cars and trucks on this road, it seems the millions spent to construct it was hardly justified. I put it down as one of those "get out the local votes highways," whereby the politicians gain more than the taxpayer. Anyway, that's neither here nor there, and after making the smooth, quick, enjoyable drive I can easily understand why the local folks would support it. Us older folks, however, would be just as content with the winding, curvy route meandering through the quaint villages, stopping along in the little country stores that popped up along the way.

We don't accept change as readily as the younger generation. I suppose that is the reason God has a set date for our demise from this old earth. If we lived forever, and kept control there would be little, if any, change. We generally like things as they are, or as they were. Often, so called progress is a losing proposition, at least in our minds. It was a good day though, and I enjoyed rambling around alone, with no destination. It's something I always loved doing but had not acted on for some time. I was reminded of how much beauty abounds in just an hour or two from me.

I always found Rockcastle to have great natural beauty and had planned on dropping by the Pine Hill cave for a brief spell, and just take a short peek inside and remember the time I spent a day in its depth. However, no matter how early one gets out and about, time is fleeting and seems the day ends before one can accomplish all the plans for that particular day. Another day soon I will venture to that cave for just a brief short walk inside. No crawling, and creeping to reach the great rooms that lie far inside the mountains. The days of that kind of adventuring are now gone, but there is great satisfaction in knowing I have already been there and done that.

Then there is the Country Music Museum at Renfro Valley. I can't believe a fan such as I have not checked it out yet. On the way back, I drove out Hwy 21 from Berea to Indian Fort. I took a brief walk and eyeballed those high bluffs Alf and I used to hike

to. Yeah, I think I can still do that. My next trip down this way will be a busy one.

Old Graveyards

From somewhere along about mid-life, I became interested in old Graveyards. I am not talking about those of recent vintage, even though I like to browse through and read the epitaphs on those also. It's the old ones I love stumbling across and thinking of those folks who left so many years ago. I find their stones and monuments to be most interesting and the epitaphs much more unusual.

Over the years I have pretty much established the fact that the longevity of family cemeteries are about two centuries. Beyond that, unless it's some historical site, or a graveyard of a family of distinction and kept under the care of a historical association, they are mostly gone forever. There is evidence of this throughout the countryside. After about two generations, old country graves are often forgotten and fall by the wayside. Stones fall, become broken, the soil, in its constant rebuilding soon reclaims the site, and the spot where someone's loved ones from long ago lay, appear as if it was never disturbed.

For some reason man cannot accept the finality of death and a monument, or crypt, or other memorial is sought to extend his existence beyond the cut off of his allotted time period. Some graves are attended for a long period of time, some not so long, but regardless, old man time conquers all, and the object set as a reminder of one that lived is no more. I suppose the living, who set those stones, also believed that it was a great act of love, and would continue to keep them connected to that person, but soon they too will lie beneath an object of art proclaiming to the world their identity and the time of their existence.

It would seem we believe in the perpetual up keeping of our honored spot, when all evidence supports otherwise. It might well be, that when the Angel's come forth and that trumpet blows, souls will rise from the Earth at some very odd locations...maybe your front yard or even the mall parking lot.

<u>Facing God</u>

Myself, along with my generation, are now getting up in the latter years. Many of our friends were not allowed to get this far. Those, we miss, and often think back on. While I hate to see the decline of energy, and the evolvement in many hectic activities that I always enjoyed, there are still many joys in life. That being said, I still enjoy living and getting old does not lessen the value of family and good friends.

I am thankful so much to have made it so far down life's highway. I think most of us think about the hereafter more often now. Especially those of us that count ourselves as believers, which I have to say I do. The end of life only means a transition from one form into another, and getting old only means we are getting closer to meeting that God that we have called on so many times. I sometimes wonder when I am called face to face with him, what will I say? Will I stammer and stutter as I try to explain some of my shenanigans on this old earth? I won't be able to lie, as the record is well recorded. He knows well enough that I have been far from perfect. There have been times I rebelled, and failed to follow through with things I should have done. There have been a few family and friends that I have inadvertently hurt or let down, and in my young days I am sure that i caused some pain in the hearts of a few young and fragile adolescent girls, just as a few of them did to me.

Those tender years can be very painful, and youth treats them callously. Yes, there were days when I was downright sinful I suppose, so when I look at Him I will have to confess. However, i was never a traitor, and for as long as I remember, I believed, and never doubted. I don't ever recall being mutinous, nor was I ever evil.

Often, I did not practice what he had preached, but when I encountered the battles between good and evil, I always tried to throw myself on the side of good. I have given many a helping hand, and I have done my best to soothe many of a sad soul with kind words and deeds.

Mostly, I have done my duty as I thought he would want it done. What he gave me, I always tried to add to, and make it better in his honor. I have no doubt about my name being in his book, even though, it may very well be down near the bottom. I will plead my case, along the lines stated above and request that this lowly person's name be allowed to remain. I will admit to him that there are many names that are more deserving of being far above mine and just being in the book of admittance is pleasing to my soul. After all, being one of the least to enter heaven's gate is no small honor. And I will humble myself in any assignment that might be forthcoming.

Tomorrow

You would think that the day you got old enough and lucky enough not to have to worry about getting up to work, one would not need to use that mysterious word tomorrow. However, no matter how old I get, I cannot delete that word of untruth from my vocabulary. I say untruth, because the phrase "tomorrow never comes" is not just an old cliché, it is, in reality true. Tomorrow has never existed, it never well. It is simply a focal point, in a short future that humans refer to as a coming point in time.

The irony is, that it never arrives. Just when old man tomorrow should appear on your doorstep, he slips in a substitute, known as today. Tomorrow is just a fantasy. It's always today in reality. Yesterday was here, we flirted and played around with him, then he went away to where, one can only guess. But tomorrow, we can wait around a million years, but he's elusive. He has never shown himself yet.

So tonight, when our clock strikes midnight, it will again be today, and old tomorrow will have once again cheated us....so that being said, I'm out of here, and will see you all tomorrow, or today, or yesterday, now I'm getting confused.

Simple Things

Been spending a little time tonight going through my thirty years of records that I've accumulated. Those, like the books I've hoarded away and collected over my lifetime, have given me much joy. There was a time that I'd travel to other states just to attend a book sale, or to some distant auctions to purchase some vintage music. In my later years those books and music have been a source of comfort. In a monetary sense there is probably little of value, as I was one to purchase what I liked, and mostly my taste ran to the common stuff.

I have a room set up to indulge in this stuff, so as not to infringe on the privacy of the family, whom have little interest, if any, of listening to Bob Wills and his Texas Playboys, wailing about hard times, complete with a heavy fiddle strain piercing the ear. Or maybe Peggy Lee belting out some early fifties Jazz. Listening tonight to some of these old forties and fifties tunes, I was once again reminded that the simple pleasures in my life had always been just that, simple. Playing an old song can often take one through a rerun of their life, and tonight was no exception. It reminded me of just how wonderful my life has been, and of how little was required to find contentment. The laughter of the children, the reading of a book in the late evening hours, or just back tripping while playing some old music, little common things can often sooth my soul.

At such times as tonight, I am reminded how blessed I was to have lived the years I did. I have to think man reached his peak, pretty much in this period of time. His innovations have skyrocketed, but from every point I look, it seems humanity is in a vast decline. The years were good to me, not perfect, but decent enough that I'd not change it. Of course, there were encounters with people, along with some other events that caused me great consternation and sorrow. Many of those, at the time I would worry about and refuse to accept, but they were things I had no control over, and could not change.

In the end, I finally gave in, and those things I perceived as negative fell in line and became part of life's pathway. It's strange now, but looking back, those events and happenings I often saw as mountains, would at a certain point become some of God's greatest gifts. Over time, those things I fretted about, they too became simple.

<u>The Book of Psalms</u>

The book of psalms is my favorite part of the Old Testament. It's easy for me to understand, as I have always loved music and poetry. No one knows for sure who composed the psalms, but it's generally agreed that the greater portion was written by David. When one reads those words from this ancient book, it's well to keep in mind that they were originally written and composed as music. That's not my take on it, but according to Biblical History, it's an accepted fact. That probably accounts for the poetic flavor that flows throughout.

This makes sense being that in his days, David was known throughout Israel as a poet and musician. His favorite Instrument was a stringed object known as a Lyre. Music was a big part in the lives of the folks that lived and praised God during Biblical days. One will find frequent references to sing praise, and also find names of various instruments such as pipes and flutes. The Harp, of course, is one of the more mentioned instruments of that time. There were percussion instruments, stringed instruments, and instruments operated by air also. An example being the rams horn.

When I was in the fourth or fifth grade, our music teacher, Mr. Hensley, gave me the assignment of reciting the 23 psalms on stage in a school play. I had to do this from memory, thus it was and is one of the reasons that I can still recite it today, and often do. Those soothing words I could never forget, and they have been a source of comfort to me from those early years. If Jewish tradition is correct, David wrote the 23rd psalms while a refugee hiding in the wilderness from King Saul and his army. Anyway, I can take the 23rd and apply it to most situations that have occurred in my life, and I could say that applies to most verses of this poetic book as well.

I have always been a mover, that's been a part of my journey since my youth. Now I don't go as much as I once did, since age has tempered my energy. Sometimes I get the feeling I am becoming tied down, but the words of the 23rd reminds me, that maybe, just maybe God's telling me it's time to lie down in green pastures, or to meander by the still waters. Maybe it's God's will, that when we reach a certain stage or age it's the best place for us to be. Be still, He's telling us. When I do have the energy to go, to move on, the 23rd lets me know that He will lead.

As mentioned earlier, being a lover of music and poetry, it's only natural that I would find the words written by the Psalmist of old comforting and inspiring. Thank God that the schools of my childhood gave me a little bit of scriptural inspiration which has followed me all the years of my life.

Life Is A Vapor

Somewhere in the Bible, I recall reading that life is but a vapor, then it's gone. I don't recall the particular verse, but I've thought of those words increasingly as I get older. I have explored different theories relating to this without coming up with the logic behind it. There is no question that when one gets into the third portion of their lives, time does accelerate quite rapidly. That particular Biblical verse explains life very well.

This Morning, being alone on the Rock House Branch, I decided to deviate from my normal routine of using the drip coffee maker and opted for the old-time percolator that sits beside my stove. Its purpose there is more for ornamental than actual usage, so I thought why not... Been a long time since I'd fired it up, so onto the burner it went. It's a slow process for sure, compared to the modern method of coffee making, but admittedly, at least to me, it makes a much more robust, hotter, and tastier cup of java.

While I awaited the heating of that brew, that old Bible verse came to mind. First, a gentle, slow vapor of steam began to rise. Then a slow boil was reached, and the vapor issued forth from the spout with more speed. When the hard-boiling point was reached, it shot upward at a much more rapid pace. I suppose this is somewhat in line with what the old prophet was speaking of when he compared it to one's life. At this point the coffee was pretty much finished. I guess that is sort of the way one's life really is.

Initially, we start out simmering slowly, then at middle age we have reached the boiling point. The molecules are rapidly changing, and when old age arises we have come to the hard boil point. We are, in effect, pretty much done. The pot is turned off, the vapor dies, the product is finished, gone, dissipated into the surrounding environment forever.

Truer words were never spoken, life is but a vapor. Hello strong coffee, you've taught me something.

Schedules

I have reached a point in my life that I hate schedules. It's the autumn years and I just want to gradually keep on ripening at a slower pace. I don't like being obligated to anyone, anything, at any time. I find it appalling, stressful, and down heartening to think I have to be anywhere on a certain date and given time, while dealing with some prearranged schedule.

I prefer to leave my future hours and days open to sudden impulse. It's not that I don't keep pretty busy for my age, but I find my days more enjoyable and more spiritually enlightening operating in this mode. When I'm relaxed, drinking my early morning cup of coffee, there's an endless possibility of subjects and events drifting through the landscape of my mind, all or none, which I may choose to act on. By the time I've had my morning shower, gotten dressed, and eaten my morning bowl of unsweetened oatmeal, I usually know what I am going to do for the next several hours, and act accordingly.

Maybe I am different, but I think most people of my age are pretty much in tune with what I am saying. It's the years we began circling the wagons, pulling the pickets in closer, and attempting to make things more compacted. We bring our families, friends, and loved ones closer inside the circle as we have become more concerned with their safety.

Sometimes though, even in advanced age, life is acted out with others. I know I have left a lot of friends perplexed when they venture forth with some idea of something we could do together tomorrow. Anyway, my reply is usually, call me in the morning about 8:30 am, then we'll see.

Tomato and Gravy

When I was a young boy, seven or eight years old, and tobacco cutting time came, an old fellow by the name of George Watkins would show up and stay with us to help with the crop.

I noticed one morning he got up from the table, went out to the garden and came back with a big tomato. He cut it, threw it on his plate along with a couple of eggs, then lapped a lot of gravy over the tomato. I thought, how odd? But like all kids, I had to try this gravy tomato thing.

George did not know it, but he had pointed me the way to one of my favorite, lifelong, culinary delights. This came in mind as we ate fried chicken, mashed potatoes and gravy tonight.

After setting down, I knew something was missing, so up I got up, went out and picked a ripe tomato, drowned it with gravy and indulged. Thank you, George, I can almost see you looking down and smiling.

A Cigar A Day

Like Abe Lincoln, the life of Winston Churchill has always fascinated me. He was himself, a strange and moody individual, who suffered from anxieties and depression to a terrible degree. As did Lincoln, yet there is no doubt but what it was Winston that preserved through those dark days of early WWII. Without him, I have little doubt that Hitler's flag would have flown from the British Isles.

I thought of him tonight as I had a cigar, which I often do after my evening meal. Wanda regulates me to the yard for that brief period, and well she should, as those things can really smell up a house. I thought of him because he was a prolific cigar smoker. He started when he was seventeen and was seldom ever encountered without that object in his hand. He said it soothed his nerves.

Until he died at the young age of ninety, it has been estimated that in his lifetime he smoked in excess of 300,000 cigars. Wanda tells me that one cigar a day will kill me...so what. 90's not a bad age to die.

<u>Aunt Jemima</u>

This morning I noticed KK having some Aunt Jemima's frozen waffles for breakfast. She likes them well, but I'm not one to advocate for a breakfast that concerns something containing so much sugar. I'd rather see her eat a healthier breakfast, but she and Wanda approved of it. I may not like it, but I've been around long enough to know there is no sense in arguing with one of the females of the species, much less taking on two. I would simply lose the argument. I'd prefer them to join me in a bowl of oatmeal, but their response would most likely be, "YUK". Maybe they're right.

Pancakes and Syrup have been a staple of the American family for years, and as far as I know it hasn't caused any great harm. In my childhood, it was the homemade version, not one you popped into a toaster. Aunt Jemima's brand, however, has been around much longer than the pancakes I ate as a youth. Since 1889 as a fact. It was originally marketed as a pancake mix, and later the Company added bottled syrup. Now days, when Wanda and KK go shopping, they have a large range of this company's products to choose from. Everything from syrup to different types of frozen meals. Even complete frozen Breakfast meals and various waffles, of all different flavors. They aren't bad, and sometimes I even opt away from my oatmeal and throw one of those frozen breakfast deals into the Microwave.

When most people prepare and indulge in one of these products, I doubt if they even know that Aunt Jemima was a real personage. I am sort of favorable to her because she was a Kentuckian, and hailed from Montgomery County, Kentucky. Her real name was Nancy Green. She was hired by the R.T. Davis Milling company in 1893 to make pancakes from the company's mix, and give away samples during the World Fair in Chicago. She would prepare over a million of them over the period of that single event. She traveled the country for more than thirty years fixing those pancakes at large events. Her image graced the packaging of their product for years. I sometimes enjoy one of her packaged breakfasts and they are always good, and in the by gone days, when I could have pancakes and syrup, it was hers that I chose. I have always been a little prejudiced towards anything made or endorsed by a Kentuckian. So, if there are going to be pancakes in the house then let it be old Aunt Jemima's.

The success of the products had a lot to do with the robust and smiling face of this women. One look at her, and you felt, now here is a happy person, a person that obviously liked to cook, and somehow that beaming black face made you know, that she was a swell cook. Over the years that smiling and happy face fixed and served several million pancakes for promotional purposes. Simply put, looking at her image made one hungry.

Like I said earlier, I still indulge in some of the products she advertised, and find them good. Sadly though, due to her appearance in the likeness of a colored servant lady, and a world of political correctness, her image has disappeared from the package. The lady that looks at me now appears more like an upper class, black house wife. She is too skinny, appears not to eat much, and one wonders if she can even cook. On top of that, her image does not make one think of food. However, times change, and the picture I envision when I pull one of those packages from the freezer, is the old time, one and only original, Aunt Jemima. Thanks to her I will continue to purchase the brand, and if KK is going to have frozen Waffles, then it's going to be those. Thankful for Aunt

Jemima (AKA Nancy Green) from Montgomery County Kentucky, for stirring me to

something delicious those many years ago. As an added note, I am thinking Nancy

Green would like me disapproving of her replacement.

<u>Light</u>

When I get up in the morning, the first thing I do is settle down with my coffee in a little recliner. I'm always up before the first rays of light begin to filter through my windows. This morning, like all mornings, there is nothing to be heard on the Rock House Branch but the sounds of nature. As I always do, I contemplate and take stock of the forth coming day. While listening to what one might say is the sounds of silence. It's this time of day that I reflect on things in general, and spiritual things in particular.

While my body, in contrast to younger days, seems to be at its frailest. My mind is always sharper and more alert. My mood is often somber and withdrawn, and I care little for early morning conversation. That is not a bad thing, as there is no one awake at that hour but me anyway. So, it is. I do a lot of meditating and thinking. I care nothing about the morning news, and don't listen or allow it to spoil my day with the endless scenes of destruction and mayhem of my fellow humans. I do, after a brief time, turn on my little weather radio. That way, I know what's in store, so I can act accordingly.

Besides the weather radio I have near my favorite chair, and within easy reach is an old-style floor lamp. That lamp is turned on before I even think of settling down with my coffee. With that lamp on, I often think, and thank Thomas Edison for its bright illumination. Light brightens my soul and lifts my spirits in those early predawn hours. I have friends and family that like dark colors, soft lights and colored walls. I am nowhere near them on this. I like white reflective walls, bright lights and less shadows. It softens my spirit, much the same way that the God given light of the Sun does.

Now, as I sit here thinking, sipping my coffee, and dwelling on what I just said about Thomas Edison's invention, it occurs to me that I am thankful to the wrong person. Sometimes, I don't think man ever invented anything. Sure, He may have twerked about with what God had already bestowed in his clockwork of nature, but invented...... I'm not sure.

The greatest light to ever befall upon the earth is that of the Sun. He took the Sun and placed it so it would give abundant light upon the entire Earth. He programmed the rotation of said Earth, so in its rotation all things upon its surface would benefit. I also think maybe God, like many of my friends, likes a little bit of soft light, so he threw in the moon to make a reflective lighting system to sooth their souls. No man-made light can ever equal the brilliance of the natural light of the Sun, and the other billions of stars of this galaxy and beyond.

However, it does not stop there. hundreds of creatures, deep in the depth of the ocean, and far beneath where the Heavenly lights reach, are equipped with their own built in cold lighting systems. Then up above, thousands of different species of fireflies have been blinking since time eternal. Electricity, invented we think, but the electric eel has been slithering around for millions of years before man ever took a step. He holds in his body 500 to 600 watts of electric to stun and kill his prey or his natural enemies. Electricity is abundant around the Earth and always has been. Static and weak sometimes, but other times powerful and destructive, such as in a major storm.

Now, we have powerfully developed sonar and radar on all our mighty warships and planes. We think that we developed it and invented it. However, the bats were using radar to navigate and hunt with long before we ever dreamed of a civilization. The Dolphins and certain Whales have traveled and hunted with the use of sonar for millions of years. We hear of, and use, Atomic power, but the Atom was the first item required in the development of the Universe. Man, merely discovered a way to split it, and in the long term, the jury is still out, on whether or not it is a good thing.

The telephone, no invention really. Sound waves have been traveling on the molecules of the air since the beginning. Alexander Bell, succeeded in performing a way for it to travel on a wire. The new wireless, just part of the beginning. Receivers pull it further, and the wireless sounds from deep space are picked up and studied by astronomers daily with the use of highly technical systems. Those distant sounds are really wireless, and come from millions of light years from Earth. Far out still, are some that are so distant, man has not developed the means to reach. Those wireless transmissions have been going on since time eternal.

Inventions, I'm not so sure we have invented anything. I could get into the cell phone and computer thing, but that would take one into the infinite domain of cells, DNA and molecules, along with atoms, and the billions of actions and storage capacity they possess. Time is wasting though, and I have to get up and about. I have to wonder though. With everything we know, have and do, in the great scheme of Gods Domain, aren't we still far below the Kindergarten level?

The Agility of a Deer

Coming from Richmond today I saw a deer. Now this is not an unusual event, as I see deer almost every day, but this particular sighting left me with a good feeling, and some thoughts on deer. I was traveling east from Richmond on the four-lane road along the Army Depot. About a quarter mile ahead I saw a deer come running out from my left near a subdivision. He was already within fifty feet of the highway and in a hard run. Obviously, he had been spooked by persons or dogs and was clearing the area and headed straight for the road.

I'm thinking this is not a good time for him to make that crossing as the time was in the late afternoon. That is when this stretch of road is very busy with traffic and today was no exception. I am also thinking that most people drive now with a phone to their ears and their vision pretty much is only concentrated straight ahead. Anyway, as my distance closed in he had reached the road and made a shot straight across. Thankfully he, or probably she, as there was no visible rack, somehow seemed to miraculously survive to reach the center of the four lanes, which consisted of a turning lane. At that point a few cars going very fast in the Eastbound lane were on her and my heart sank as I could see no way a collision could be avoided, but at that precise second the deer just slightly lost its footing. I was amazed at how quick it regained its balance and shot on across the other two lanes.

Fortunately for the animal, and probably the few cars involved, that slight mishap of his hoof slipping, gave a split-second chance for the cars nearest him to fly on by. I was at that point, very close and saw the deer clear those two lanes and hit the grass on the depot side. I felt good to see it survive and an accident avoided. The agility of that deer was amazing. Across that entire four lane it appeared his leaps were far enough that it appeared its hoofs only touched down four or five times, at most. On that slick asphalt he slightly slipped only once, and recovered so fast, that if I had not been watching intently, that slip would have not been noticed. In the traffic, and running at full speed, it displayed an amazing amount of grace. I was relieved, as I am sure a few other drivers, whom I'd seen braking, were as well.

It was then that my heart sank again as I watched the deer come upon the depot fence. My first thought was, he is trapped and without any place to go. He will have to reverse course, and run the gauntlet back across that road. My concern was unwarranted, because the deer never gave that fence a second thought. He started his jump several feet away and the leap carried him handily over without as much as a single foot touching. I said jump, but I have seen deer enough over the years to question if they ever jump. What they do is simply take flight and gracefully float over obstructions. I assume that the fence in question here is at least six feet tall with three strands of barb wire on top of that.

Touching the ground on the other side it's gait never faltered and it bounded on. By then, I was going past and saw it go out of sight into some bushes inside the Depot area. Though it caused me a little apprehension, I was delighted, after the fact, to have witnessed the scene.

I started thinking about deer in general. I have seen them chased by dogs, and know for a fact a deer can often leap twenty feet or possibly more when fleeing from danger. They are one of the most graceful of God's creatures. I have always been amazed to see a buck with a large rack run through woods and brush without getting entangled in all the materials he runs through. Today was a good show, and it turned out well. I always wondered how high a deer can jump. After today, I think they can jump as high as they need to.

<u>Wildcat</u>

Wildcat died a few days ago. There was no big memorial service, no visitation, no funeral of any kind. I simply put him in a little box, and placed him out in the back yard. It's there where so many furry friends from years gone by, now lie.

The Grand kids were the ones who appropriately named him Wildcat. The name was well deserved. He had been around for several years, but always at a distance. I'd sit in the yard, late in the evening, and see him come from the woods. He'd never come close, but would sit there within a few feet of those woods and study me. His eyes were always focused and alert. I would try calling him, but no amount of coaxing would bring him near a human. The few times I tried to approach him, he'd simply take flight back into his wild domain to be seen no more that day. Even though he was wild, I always suspected that he came out late at night, and fed on what little cat food was left after the tame cats had ate on the back deck. Sometimes we'd go weeks without seeing him, but when he'd make those few, few trips to the edge of our lawn, I would always put just a tad more food out. He was a large feline, being orange and white in color. Just by his haughty disregard for humans and the way he survived in those dark woods behind my house, one could sense, here was a mammal that pretty much existed in the days of yore. Those days beyond, and before the Gods of Egypt had domesticated his forefathers.

The years went by, and then for several months there was no sign of him. I missed seeing him stroll by in the brush, with just a glimpse when he would drift into a cleared spot here and there, his head always up and straight, moving in a half-crouched position as the primitive cats of the wild often walk. One day last winter, when the temperature dropped into the single digits for a spell, I went out on the deck to feed my cats. I notice a bundle of fur from the corner of my eye and there on the top steps stood Wildcat. I say stood, but it was more of a crouch than a stand. It took a few minutes to recognize him. That haughtiness and wild look of independence was gone. He was skinny, hair terribly matted, and appeared very unhealthy. That look of disdain and pride no longer showed in his eyes. I approached him, placed some food before his face, and he never moved. He showed only resignation, and despair, but as I backed away I saw him slowly lower himself to eat.

It struck me that wild cat had given up to seek help. He had gotten old, and like his human counterpart, had to face the fact that it was time for an old folk's home. I put together a little box, insulated it, and placed it in a corner on my deck and there he took up habitation and seldom left it. He would come out for food and water, and the occasional rest room use, but usually after I left the porch. He seemed happy there, and gained some of his health back. Even the Grand kids could rub his back, and even though he appeared to like it, it was more of a final acceptance than anything else. Often when the sun came out he would lay and look longingly for hours towards the coolness and shade of those woods that had been his home so long. But when late evening came, with one final look in that direction, he would crawl into his little house and sleep for hours. He knew his independence was over, and seemed to grudgingly accept it.

Yesterday I put the cat food out and noticed he was nowhere around. I wondered but knew it my heart, and had accepted it from day one, that he was a short timer or he'd never have surrendered his freedom. I figured he had went off and died, never to be seen again. This morning I went under the little shed on the back of my garage to retrieve a tool I had left there. Looking around I saw a bundle of yellow and white laying up on a tool shelf. I did not have to investigate, I knew before hand it was old Wildcat. I found a box, went back, wrapped him in a towel, then silently laid him in the soil alongside Alfie, Cookie and a dozen or more other friends that I've had to put away over the years.

I dreaded telling my Grand Daughter KK, so I put it off and decided to let her bring it up, should she miss him. I need not have worried. With four other cats and four dogs on the place she never brought it up. When she went to feed the cats with me today her only comment was," Pappaw, Wildcat is not here, I bet he has went back to live in the woods." I replied, "Yes, Honey, yes, I think that is exactly what he did." For once, I thought, maybe, just maybe he did. It would be just like him to be wild again.

Infinity

It's January 4th, 2017, and of course, the beginning of a New year. The time is about 10 PM and I have found myself outside, picking up a few pieces of wood to replenish the wood box. It's much colder tonight than it has been lately. I find myself looking heavenly, and was mildly surprised to notice that the clouds have moved on, and the night sky is displaying much brilliance. The stars are at their best showing tonight and the Heavens are a sight to behold. That is one of the advantages of being in the country. There, one is away from the artificial lights of towns and subdivisions, not to mention street lights, car lights and other forms of electric lights. Therefore, the night sky always shows its natural lights to the best advantage. Tonight, there appears to be a couple of thousand stars visible to my naked eyes. For a moment it enters my mind to start counting, but years of stargazing and admiration of the same has taught me the futility of such an endeavor.

I already know that in our little galaxy known as the Milky Way, our Sun, has in the Neighborhood of 150 billion brothers and sisters. The Milky Way itself is not a lone Galaxy, it occupies and shares the vastness of space with about 10 trillion other galaxies. The scientific world is in agreement that the numbers are far beyond what they have previously estimated. Now, ten trillion galaxies are a lot of galaxies, and considering that the average number of stars in a galaxy is somewhere between 100 billion to 200 billion, the numbers stagger one's mind. It would appear that to be exact, there are about 10,000,000,000,000,000,000,000,000 known stars. Well not exactly, as there is little known to be exact in time and space, but a pretty good scientific guess.

These amounts are so comprehensive, that they can create in one's mind, the idea that his miniaturization makes him very insignificant indeed. When I look or study on all the grandeur of the heavens, I am always struck with the thought that I could never have been an astronomer, physicist or any other profession that deals with the study of time and space. The vastness of the numbers, distances and time would drive my small brain insane. Unlike the learned men of science, who are always looking for a beginning and end, I always look on this as infinity, without either.

Some would look at my view as anti-religious, but I see it otherwise. After all, my God, as I understand him, is forever. I cannot conceive of him ever having a beginning. He Himself is the beginning and the end. Has always been and will always be. From the majesty of the universe it would have been simple for Him to ball up a little rock and soil it in his fist and throw it into orbit, thus creating a little work of art known as the Earth. One of his better masterpieces. The more I see of the discoveries made daily by science, the more I see a universal intelligence alive and well. I am not trying to sell anyone on any Ideological opinions, but when I look and study the skies I see magic on a grand scale.

Now, anyone that knows me, knows well enough, that I am not smart enough to come up with such figures as I am putting forth here, let alone solve the riddles of time and space. However, they also know that I read a lot, and what I read encompasses a large area of subject matter. I may read science today and fiction tomorrow. There is little that does not interest me. Therefore, my brain is pretty much filled with mostly useless trivia. As a matter of fact, the large numbers I have quoted herein come from something I have read in the not so distant past, and may themselves be off somewhat. After all my mind is a lot slower now than in former years, but I don't think anyone will care, since most of these numbers are too vast for I, or most of my friends, to comprehend anyway. Besides, when it comes to universal space, what's a few trillion here and there?

However, books on the complexities of space can be very hard to read or understand, but fortunately there are many put out for the benefit of the dummies such as I. One of my favorites would be Stephen Hawking, "The Universe in A Nutshell." Mr. Hawking's attempts, and in my case succeeds, in writing a book that the laymen can grasp and understand. There is also Carl Sagan's volume called "Comets". An excellent look at the often overlooked and ignored mystery of the billions and billions of pieces of renegade space material that answers to no patterns, but runs their endless gauntlet, defiant of all known rules of behavior and in direct contradiction of the fixed planetary systems that make up the various galaxies.

My latest addition to my reading list for us laymen, is a fellow by the name of David Blatner. Mr. Blatner can take one on a journey through the magic of the universe in a simple and understanding manner. He also tends to deal with subjects that are stellar related, but which, also lie at our fingertips. His latest book is called "Spectrums". He looks at the colossal things of the universe but can and does regress to the most miniature objects that we know to exist. One will find many interesting bits of information in spectrums, from the temperature that oxygen freezes, (yes, oxygen does have a freezing point, let's hope it doesn't get that cold.) to the temperature of the Sun and other stars. Blatner also uses a study by Scientists at the University of Hawaii, to answer that age-old question. Which is more? The grains of sand on the Earth, or the number of stars in the heavens? While I am not going to explain, nor attempt to look at the formula they came up with, which I, nor my friends would understand anyway, suffice it to say, that the stars won handily.

Anyway, one is getting into such numbers as quintillions and quadrillion's which means nothing to us down to earth people. Numbers mean little in the infinity of space, and with the Hubble telescope and various other satellite technology, they change daily in large numbers. So, I attempt to learn about deep space, which in turn makes me feel like I, and yes, the earth and even our Milky Way, is so small in relation to the rest of space, we really don't matter. Then when I come across "Spectrums" I get sucker punched. No big deal about there being so many stars says Blatner, after all, if you take just ten drops of tap water you will find the number of H_2o molecules so vast, that they themselves outnumber the stars of Heaven.

One soon realizes that God did not just go into infinity at the top, but infinity exist at the bottom also. Numbers in atoms, molecules, etc., in the smallest items of materials, at the lowest level of the spectrum, most often outnumber those vast, unbelievable numbers that we see relative to universal space. Somehow, I am not sure why, but this makes me feel somewhat better. I know few care, or seldom think, about the subject matter i just put forth, but a few moments of skygazing took me out into far-left field. I am going to have to quit looking up when I am outside at night. It can be trying to one's mind.

September Weather

It's September, the twenty second, 2017. I really don't know where Summer has gone, but it certainly seems it was brief enough. I am a little shocked at seeing how much the leaves have turned. I suppose it's time, but it does seem just a tad early to see them start falling, which they are doing. Deciding to get out and about, I did something I seldom do. I broke out the old ATV and headed up a remote area that we refer to at Mistletoe, as The Campbell Fork. The Sun was out, the sky clear, and little, if any, humidity hung about. I have not been up this fork of Buffalo Creek in many years, even though it lies only a few miles from where I stay. In younger times it was a favorite Camping spot for my friends and I, and truly is one of the more scenic and remote areas of the Daniel Boone Forest. There was a time in my youth when many families lived here, but the purchase by the Forest Service in the late fifties and sixties created mostly what today is a Wild and scenic area. I am not much for ATV riding because one misses too much, and the sound itself, is a distraction.

I have always preferred to hike, but the hiking is not that easy anymore, and to pretend otherwise is to deny the frailty of one's body at seventy years of age. I still do walk, but walking and hiking are two different ways of getting around. Walking is what one does on soft and easy trails. Hiking is what is required in rougher country, and there are some rough places where I went today. I have had an ATV for many years, and at different times, but in all probability, I have never ridden over fifty miles in all those years. Looking at the scenery from astride that four-wheeler made me think of just how disappointed my late little dog Alf would have been. He was a hiker and hated ATV's. That was in contrast to the little Cocker Spaniel that was my companion previous to Alf. She adored riding, but would only ride astride the gas tank and between my legs. It was a tenacious position and I had to be very gentle operating that machine. Making a seat with a cushion on the front rack and the back rack did not change her mind. It was still the Gas Tank she chose. I ended up gluing a piece of carpet over part of the tank, and her little toes clamped strongly, and we could move along at a good pace. I thought of those two long gone pals, and how much we enjoyed September. Now, however, I was looking and meditating alone.

September is a month I have never been sure of. It's supposed to announce the death of Summer, and the arrival of Autumn. However, in Kentucky, the days can sometimes be as hot as those of July and August. Other times it can consist of cool nights and cooler days. Regardless, I love September. It's a time of ripening, and the fruit is succulent as it falls to the ground. I had just demonstrated this to myself as I had just eaten a nice ripe pear from an old tree back down the road a piece. I was also now engrossed in trying to locate a Pa-paw tree, but having little luck. I might very well be too late on those. The fields and meadows of September are even more beautiful than the woods. The Trees have not nearly reached their full range of colors, but the bottom lands are flush with beauty. Chicory, Goldenrod, Black Eyed Susan and hundreds of others are now on display. So, as I regard this month of my birth, I am also reminded that September, with all it positives, beauty and goodness, is sort of a paradox. It leaves one with a good feeling, a closeness with nature, but at the same time the knowledge,

that it's also a signal that many things in the plant and insect kingdom are very shortly

going to die. Nonetheless, It's my time of year. If I could have picked a month to be born

in, it would have been this one. I've enjoyed my day with you September, so roll on, and

exit as the Queen you truly are.

The Finish

The years have slipped up on me. I am now old enough to realize that I have been incredibly blessed to have achieved the status of Senior Citizenship. I have lots of friends older, but any, or all of us, could safely say when our hour comes, we died of old age. No matter how the Coroner views it.

In my case I have enjoyed the trip, and would not change anything. Even if I could and was able to change any episode, I would not. The changing of one minute in one's past, would have dire consequences for the entire play. Every little moment is intertwined with the whole, and the script would be altered in some way or another. I think it was Shakespeare who said that the entire World was a stage, and we, merely the Actors. I think that is a pretty fair description. In my case I see the play coming to an end in the not so distant future. Anyway, what's a few more years, a few more months, or a few weeks for that matter. The audience is getting bored, and the lines I'm quoting are beginning to become monotonousness. The theatrical crew is set to pull the curtains. In both groups and single file, the patrons are exiting. I, and my fellow actors have played our parts. The great play writer, and director have kept me in to the finish. Some of my fellow actors were written out and removed from the cast early.

I'm honored that I have gotten to stay in until the final run. I feel the season was a success. I delivered my lines the best I could, and I performed the best I knew how. Throughout it all, and up until the finish, I'm still not sure if I played in a comedy or a tragedy, but I'm thinking it was mostly a mixture of both. Anyway, at this point I feel it matters little. What does matter, is that I was allowed to play, and I feel I played my part well.

The Truth

Now that I've gotten old, I find myself sitting here reflecting back on my life about what I saw as good and true. Mostly, the answers I get are things and events of little significance. I realize that mostly what I experienced as good and truth, were not things I learned in school or some college classroom. I found it mostly in the folks I met along the way. I found it on the highways and byways of America during the late sixties when I dropped out like many other young people.

To seek something different, but never knowing what it was we searched for. I'd discovered truth even earlier in my parents, and the parents of my friends, whom were mostly poor, and lowly educated.

Regardless, they gave it their all and put family, children and country above themselves. I saw it in the company of hundreds of young nomads, complete with back packs, and occasionally a guitar, as they thumbed their way across the continent in those turbulent sixties. I noticed it around their campfires while some straight-haired hippie chick strummed her instrument and sang her song. While at the same time praying for a change in the affairs of mankind. A few times I found it in a late night smoky bar room while I danced cheek to cheek with a pretty lady whose name I did not know, nor would I ever. I discovered it sometimes in a dark and secret lover's lane with a pretty young girl, who would share their thoughts and souls, while alone and away from the world.

I saw it crop up in faraway lands as well. Lands such as the Philippines, as I watched dark eyed Senoritas do their dance, and felt my spirits lifted by their laughter and happiness. I saw it crop up on various backpacking trips as I mingled and shared my camp with young, vibrant, free spirited individuals who were total strangers. I learned at an early age, it existed with the old men I fished with as we waded and threw our baits along the rapids of the South Fork river.

I even saw it a few times in the Winos whom i encountered sleeping on the Sidewalks of South Chicago and other cities, with nothing but a Newspaper for cover. Sometimes, it would show itself in the truck drivers that would take time to gear their big rigs down and give my bone-weary body a lift. Later I'd find it in a pretty seventeen-year-old, whom I ended up making a life long journey with. I saw it in the two little bundles of joy she gave to me, and later the little grand bundles. Mostly what I discovered about good and truth was that it most often came from the middle class, to the bottom of Society. I discovered that the higher up one advanced on the chain of humanity, the less good and truth one encountered. Mostly, the good and truth, as it relates to my life, has been the everyday plain old common folks.

Halloween

Well, in a few days it's going to be Halloween. After seeing all the little children dressed as ghosts to attend their school or some other party, it's only natural that it would be on my mind. I am sort of like old Ebenezer Scrooge in a way. The Holiday, (if one can call Halloween a Holiday), that I think on now is one of those in the far past.

The past several years has shown me a great improvement on the way that this occasion is celebrated. I guess I first noticed this last fall when I drove from Clay County to Richmond on Halloween eve. It was already dark, and I made the trip without anything out of the ordinary happening. In the East Kentucky Counties I grew up in as a young man, this would probably not have happened. Most of my teen years were in Oneida, in Clay County, and this night, was truly, the "Devils Night." It was looked forward to and anticipated far in advance. By the time the night arrived dozens of young men would band together, and their night of mischief would begin. I think Oneida was the worst for the pranks and shenanigans. Most of the night these young people would be out tipping over outhouses, blocking roads by sawing down trees, pulling debris across the rural highways, and many other instances of dragging old cars across the road, and dozens of other kinds of mischief, and yes, even a little vandalism. Thirty or Forty years ago, one would have to be a little senile to attempt travel on this night of hideous activities. One never knew what kind of mayhem may occur.

Along after daylight, one could hear the occasional chainsaws fired up as the early commuters cleared out the mess. That day would also see a lot of the Transportation Departments workers spending their time cleaning up. Prior to that day of cleanup, Halloween eve would have seen the little trick or treaters make their rounds from house to house, mostly by automobile. This was done well before ten PM, so as to be off the road, before the big boys began their high-spirited activities. Later as Adults, Wanda and I would always stock up on candy for those little tricksters, and enjoy their coming to our door. Times have changed, and even though the past few years I have made sure to have a few treats on hand, no tiny goblins have shown up. This Halloween tradition has pretty much ceased to exist in the rural areas with the exception of some of the bigger subdivisions.

The craziness of some in today's society has caused this harmless activity to occur now only at shopping malls and business due to safety concerns. A sad thought, but one of reality. In our World now, a child cannot accept candy from a stranger, even if it is passed out from a 911 address. On the plus side, the blocking of roads, the light vandalism, and the other mean-spirited activities have mostly disappeared. People began to take notice of the dangers involved in cutting trees across a road way. The blocking could well, well cost lives if an emergency vehicle needed access somewhere. Much like the attention that drunk drivers finally received, so did that of dangerous acts during Halloween.

While I too, did my part on those nights of the macabre, I have to say I am glad to see the new era that came forth some years back. The older kids now attend, and in many cases, help put on the Haunted Forest, The Grave Yard Meadows, the Haunted houses, and hundreds of other fearful places.

It is a sign that some things have gotten better. Halloween eve is certainly one. So, set tight, enjoy this Halloween, and keep safe from all those awesome ghosts, hideous creatures, and horrid personalities that only venture forth this one night out of the year. After all, surely, we can allow them one solitary night to spew forth their ghastly, gruesome, and horrid features. Just a brief period, and they will fade away for another twelve Months.

<u>Cracker Jacks</u>

It's not often that Wanda and I get a chance to just set down and chat together. When we do she usually has to listen to me talk about the old days, or of times past concerning a memory that has recently come to pass. She's always telling me how amazed she is that I can remember such trifling episodes that I bring up. She recalls very few things from her young childhood. She simply does not remember happenings that occurred in her young time frame that correlates to the same time frame in mine. Honestly, sometimes, for whatever reason, I feel she must have blocked them out.

I had Cracker Jacks on my mind today, and inquired of her if they still made this popcorn candy. I also asked her if the box it came in contained a cheap toy. That too was a positive. I must say I was mildly surprised to learn that they still existed. Cracker Jacks were on my mind because I had been recalling earlier in the day how popular this product was with us children of the fifties. There were few sweets in the old country stores, but this little box of nifty sweetness was always available.

I related to her about the time when I, as a little bare foot boy of about seven or eight, was walking down the old dusty road of Buffalo Creek. I stepped off to the side of the road when I heard an old Jalopy approaching. The old guy driving that ancient vehicle stopped and gave me a lift. The first thing I noticed when I settled into the old worn out leather seat, was that he was eating a box of Cracker Jacks. Now, I was never one to beg, but I sure was hoping he'd pass that box to me and say, "here young fellow, have a bite", or some other words to that effect. However, nothing of the sort happened, and in a short time we had covered the brief distance to my house. Stopping, I opened the door to get out. Upon my exit he spoke up as he discarded the empty box into the floor, where numerous other pieces of trash had previously been deposited. "I sure am sorry young fellow, I plumb forgot to offer you some of my Jacks." I had been disappointed, but I was never one to hold a grudge.

I knew too well how hard it was for a young kid to come up with the five cents to buy a box of these goodies. Being just a kid, I assumed it was probably just as hard for him to acquire the means to purchase. Nonetheless, I must say, I was glad to find out Cracker Jacks are still around but I doubt if they bring anywhere near the excitement they did to a young kid of the fifties. Cracker Jacks, like many name brands of today, have been around for a lot longer than I have. In the case of this once popular candy, it dates back to 1872, when a German Immigrant by the name of F.W. Rveckheim, mixed a concoction of popcorn, molasses and peanut butter together, and began selling it at his Chicago popcorn stand. I'm sure he was probably not the first to make this mixture, but, he was the first to figure out a formula to keep it from sticking together in big globs. Finding it to be a bigger seller than his regular popcorn, he then invented a means of making a wax sealed box. This genius of an idea allowed it to be kept for long periods of time, and assured it a long shelf life. He then began marketing it to various stores.

It was just a matter of time until the giant retailer Sears and Roebuck picked it up, and in 1902 it could be purchased through their catalog. The rest is history. However, what really sold the product was the inclusion of a cheap toy in every box. It was every child's dream, to be able to get a box of candy, and a surprise toy in every box. It's been a stable marketing gimmick ever since, and used often by other companies. Witness today's fast food giant McDonald's, and their kid's Happy Meals. Kids will whine to get that Happy Meal because it comes with a cheap toy.

In 1919 Mr. Rveckheim hired an artist to put a cover on the box. The subject used by the artist was the owner's grandson and his little dog Bingo. That picture of the little Sailor and his dog graced the cover of the box for years, and as far as I know, still does. The little grandchild, though, never got to see his picture, as he died from a flu-like illness just a few months before the new box design came out. I never knew the history of Cracker Jacks when I was a kid. As a matter of fact, I just researched it today, after Wanda and I had a discussion about that early candy. Many times, the history on a subject can be much more entertaining than the item one is writing about. I'd venture to say there are many old timers like me, who are thankful to Mr. Rveckhelm for developing and marketing an item that gave us so much pleasure in our youth. The next time I'm out, I am going to purchase myself a box of Cracker Jacks and indulge.

I am skeptical, though, that there will be anywhere near the taste and thrill of yesterday. There are simply too many items out there now to placate one's palate. Regardless, I will be forever mindful and appreciative of that little sailor boy, and his dog, Bingo, who guided me to something so tasteful and delicious those many years ago. It did not hurt that they also guided me to a wonderful little surprise to go along with that treat.

Bibliophiles

A short time back I drove up to Frankfort to see my good friend Larry Arnett. He'd been after me to come up for some time, but because of the hot summer weather I kept putting it off. Finally, a brief cool down made my mind up, so out I headed. I probably should have called and given some sort of advance notice, but that would have been against my old age policy of never planning my days ahead. I just sort of flow with the mood when I get up and about, then when I am fully alert, I decide what my forth coming day is going to consist of.

If by chance Larry and his wife Mary, were not home, I'd simply take in a few sights and scenes of Frankfort, call it a lazy day, and return home. Of course, I'd probably be disappointed, as these two, wonderful people have been friends for so many years, it would be hard to remember the exact date when that friendship began.

Now Colonel Arnett has a disease, and that is another reason I held my visit up. You see, he is a bibliophilist. It's a dreaded thing to be stricken with and I am afraid he contacted it from me many years ago. I am sure Mary has cursed me for these many times since. I try to avoid bibliophiles anymore, as they often are possessed with many books, of which I cannot resist. Since Larry had confided in me several months back that he was in the process of cutting down his stash of treasures, and invited me to come forth and partake first choice, I thought it best to stay away. I was proud of myself for getting rid of part of my stash a few years ago, but in all honesty, it seems to be increasing again, and I felt sure if I made the trip, I could not refuse.

Now, book lovers are an endangered species, so that leaves us old folks who have read, loved, and admired books, in a dilemma of sorts. We have no one to pass them down to, so we are apt to push them to some library or best choice, some friend. The technology world has upended and overthrown the staple of America's entertainment. Good books, lovingly read, by some bedside light, until one's eyelids become heavy with sleep, are long gone the byways. It's no mystery to me why insomnia is out of control.

Anyway, I happened to be searching for one of my prized books, and nowhere could I find it. Several days of searching, I became desperate and called Larry. Yes, he had a duplicate, and would be glad to give it to me. I suppose mine had went the way of so many others over the years. It had been loaned out, and loaned books have a way of never returning. One of the parties, or possibly both, would forget, and the orphan book is gone forever. I had to have that book, so off to Frankfort I went. Going up the Interstate I kept repeating, "just the one book, that's all I need," until I figured I had it drilled in my brain well enough.

Well, so much for hypnosis, I soon found myself barreling back down said interstate with about four large crates. He had reinfected me with that dreaded disease. How could I refuse? Many were very old and ancient, and it's those I am addicted to the worst. Old books take up a lot of my living space, and when company drops in, I usually have to start moving them from couches and chairs in order to create a sitting space.

Old books have a pleasing smell, or odor. Often inside will be inscribed the name of a former owner, sometimes a hundred years or even longer. They are treasures, and it breaks my heart to see them defaced, marked up, torn, or thrown away. I view the defacing of a good book as a crime.

The ones most guilty of defacing and damaging these works of art, are the very people that are supposed to preserve and protect them. So, it is that libraries are the worst to damage good books. They stamp, glue cardholders, mishandle, and show little respect towards what they are supposed to preserve. Anyway, this day I returned with some jewels. A few first edition Mark Twain's, although in poor condition, loved by me nonetheless. A few early Lew Wallace, and some early poetry, by many of the great poets of the last two centuries.

While I find the old English poets hard to read at times, I was delighted with an ancient copy of Shelley's works, edged with gold guilt, and beautifully illustrated. He is one of the few old English poets that I truly love to indulge in from time to time. Reading Shelley though, I'd recommend one only spend a few hours a week, as often his works can lead one down a path to depression. His work often dwells with death and dying. He was certainly sort of a depressed individual, as many of the great poets were. Such words as, "first our pleasures die, then our hopes, then our fears, and when these are dead, the debt is due, dust claims dust, and we die too," certainly did not come forth from a happy individual. Thankfully, though, old Shelley did at times come forth with more enlightening material.

Anyway, I am sitting here, and a pile of The Colonel's books surround me. They are heaped up, taking the remaining room on the opposite end of my couch. In the floor are several boxes, not yet unpacked. I am contemplating where to put them, but have come to no conclusion as of yet. However, these are great gifts, from a great friend, and will be treated accordingly.

I thank Larry very much for this treasure trove, but it's obvious, some more of my former stuff will have to go. It's a never-ending cycle. Oh, the curse of being a bibliophile.

Recalling Thanksgiving Past

Well, Its official. There will be no big Thanksgiving Dinner at my House. Wanda and I will be visiting my Daughter and eating there. The big meals she has cooked for over forty years are over. I guess this is sort of a victory for me in a way. Over many Thanksgivings I have been pointing out the fact that our big meals are pretty much wasted. Holidays she always worked hard, both the day before, and the actual day of the feast. She would be cooking, baking, roasting and fixing enough food for dozens of people. That was just fine back in the day, but times have changed. It's been years since we have had a large group of family and friends to drop by on this special day. Our kids may drop by briefly and grand kids may be in attendance, but the pitiful small amount they eat does not justify the large effort that is put forth. Besides, they had probably just as soon eat a pizza.

The old-time foods have little appeal to most of the modern-day generation. Then one is faced with the hours of clean up, and then storing the food in the frig. I may indulge in left overs for a day or so, but ultimately, a great portion of the feast will be devoured by our two outside dogs.

I guess there is some satisfaction that they enjoy the feast, but have no knowledge of why this wonderful surplus fell into their hands (or paws rather). They are however, very thankful I'm sure. The reason she cooked those large meals: tradition. A tradition that both she and I grew up around. Thus, it was that we followed, and tried to keep alive the beauty and appreciation of our blessings. We went so far into our adulthood, after the fad faltered, we refused to give in until now.

Thanksgiving through the many generations, especially of rural America, was a glorious event. It was a time when the Siblings would arrive from distance States and Cities to spend several days with the old folks. The aged parents and grandparents would literally bask with pride and joy with having their Children and grandchildren around. Families were close and special in those days. Unlike many today, they were well aware that there were, in fact, many things to be thankful for. No matter how poor they were they gave thanks for what they had, and shared it as a blessing with all who wished to come visit and partake.

I myself, spend a lot of time during the Holidays of Christmas and Thanksgiving, remembering how special they were. Today, it's not about the Holidays. It's about Black Friday sales, Christmas sales and commercial events. We can't even get through Thanksgiving, because we are too busy thinking about Christmas. To the point that we are putting Christmas before the Thanksgiving Holiday even has time to arrive. Even worse, we push Christmas back for the wrong reasons. Just can't wait to go pull out the plastic and create more debt for the year to come. We have become creatures of material things, and the spiritual side of humanity has lost much.

The years I remember, Wanda and I would have to have our Dinner a few days before Thanksgiving, so we could travel back home, and have a big turkey meal with her Parents. Then following that, we were expected to then go to visit my Parents, and eat there as well. One had to be prepared to eat a lot of food, or the host would be quite disappointed. A few days following the feast, the children and grandchildren would make ready to head back to their jobs, and homes in some far-off place. There would be many tears on the wrinkled and weathered faces of parents and grandparents. The children, too, would be hanging on with hugs and moist eyes.

If you are one that expects a large crowd of family, and are fortunate enough to have them show. Hopefully you will be lucky enough that you can keep everyone off of their phones from texting, interacting with social media, game systems and other distractions, and they actually show love and interaction, then you should be exceedingly Thankful. Good Luck with that, and Happy Thanksgiving!

<u>Some Childhood Thoughts</u>

For whatever reason, I am stuck in my childhood tonight. This is an infrequent thing but it does happen. Other times I may get into one of those moods where I dwell in my teen years. Whatever period my mind settles in, I always react in some form or another.

In the case of childhood, I normally conjure up forgotten scenes of early childhood. In the case of the teen years, it usually leads me to a desire to replay and listen to old music, especially those great tunes of the fifties and sixties. Practically every old song will bring a fond memory, or in a few cases, a sad one. They are almost always connected to a person, place or event from many years past. Old songs bring back Memories of some young girls, or some good friends, or some distant places I once resided in. It may even bring back old ships, old dance halls, taverns or vehicles that I once drove. Whatever it pulls back to the fore front, it is always something or an event that is no longer accessible and now long out of reach.

Tonight, though, it is my very small childhood that is playing on the windows of my mind. I am always amazed at the inconsequential things that come to mind, such as a few scenes of being a child on the old mountain farm. I have thought tonight of bringing the cow in. If one said today they had to go bring the cow or cows in, I am sure most would not know what you were talking about. However, any farm lad that was a child during the period I grew up would well know, and probably have done it themselves.

Now, I am being slightly dishonest to say I brought the cow home. I was too young for Dad to send me on such an errand alone. That task was most always given to my older brothers, Wayne and Albert, but seeing it as an adventure, I was often allowed to tag along. If the two older boys didn't do the job, then it fell to Dad, and with him I practically followed every footstep he made. It was an adventure, and one may encounter snakes, chiggers, lizards, grouse, and a dozen other kinds of wildlife. Sometimes the old bovine would be close, but other times she would be far up the mountain. You simply listened until every now and then you would hear the sound of her bell and point your direction to it. Once located she usually came home easy enough, and one just ambled along behind and let her take the lead. If it was late in the evening, she seemed to walk reluctantly and uncomfortably, as her udders were hanging and very engorged, needing the relief that only milking was going to bring at that point. If it was winter, the cow hunt was seldom necessary, as there was little forage, and the cold mountain temps usually kept her near the barn. She was glad to be there early, as during that period her food supply was connected to the humans and the barnyard. The idea of a little shelter from the cold nights was no doubt a big incentive also.

In the winter, it was always a big thrill to get on the old horse drawn sled, and ride with my father to the coal banks. Another word no one hears today, but in those times a coal bank was practically a part of every homestead. Coal was primarily the main heat for most people on Buffalo. Coal which was dug by their own hands, and collected, hauled, and piled by their own hands, and maybe the aid of a mule or horse. I absolutely loved the coal banks. It usually involved auguring and setting off a stick of dynamite, which I found highly exciting. My father would set me over the bank behind a pile of mine spoil, then go light the fuse, he'd then jump over to shelter beside me, and soon would come that big muffled boom. We'd leave our concealment and enter a scene of dense smoke and the acrid smell of burned powder.

My Mom and Dad used to laugh and tell me I'd sometimes wake up at three or four-o-clock during the night crying to go to the coal bank. What little it took to satisfy the mind of a young toddler of those days. Sometimes, I still walk to where that little coal bank existed just to relive some happy moments. There were plentiful activities for a young child growing up on that creek. We hunted and collected Walnuts, Hickory nuts, Hazelnuts, and scores of other wild forges that we used for human consumption. Of course, there were the Possum Grapes, the Summer Grapes, Blackberries, Mountain Tea, and other natural growing food items. The Mountain Tea we just chewed for its pleasant taste, much like one chews gum today.

I loved my childhood, and I find it comforting. Somehow, though, it makes me sad that it doesn't exist anymore. The children of today are indoor mostly, addicted to comforts and electronics. I feel like our society has lost much.

Winters of Yester Years

It's the second day of the New Year. 2018 to be exact. The eastern and northern parts of the country are under a blanket of intense cold. One might say a lot of the south, also, as this front has made a large dip in that direction.

I don't tolerate the cold as I once did, so I am impatient to see this Canadian visitor go back north. This is really what I remember of the winters of my youth. I am afraid the past several years in Kentucky, we have become spoiled as it relates to mild weather. True, we have had a few really cold days each winter, but the period of deep freeze has been brief, and its duration lasted a week or so.

Driving this morning, I noticed all the creeks and streams are frozen white. That is the way most of us who were children in the !950's remember the streams and rivers appearing all winter long. The creeks and rivers of my childhood are still imprinted on my mind as being white and frozen. That made for a lot of fun as we walked the ice-covered creek to and from school. To us kids playing on that ice, the zero temps, and frozen waters had little impact on our life, and was accepted as what it was. Just plain all winter weather. The difference was that in those days it was a pretty sure bet that nothing was going to change until Spring.

I suppose the grown-ups had it tougher, but I don't recall any complaining. As a matter of fact, I don't recall folks discussing the weather like they do today. It was what it was, and beyond one's control, so you dealt with it and went on with the everyday routine of living a mountaineer's life.

There were four Seasons in those days and they were each very distinct. There was tough and thick ice also, and it would readily hold us kids as we skated and jostled on its surface. Snow too, could come and sometimes be heavy. Unlike today, it could often lay deeply over the earth for weeks, or even a few months.

I think any of us my age or close to it has to admit there is a warming of our weather patterns, and it's been going on for about as long as our memories go back. As cold as it was in my young days, winters were much worse and colder in each of the preceding generations. To hear those old men back in the fifties, talk about hauling loads of logs by Oxen across the South Fork River when they were young lads, made for some interesting listening.

We can point to this cold temperature as proof against the global warming people's position, but those who read history, and those of us in advanced age, have to agree that the seasons are running together now. Yes, we get record breaking chills, but they are scarcer and of a much shorter period of time. This one may prove me wrong as it's got a pretty good grip, but I am hoping that it, like others nowadays, will be short lived. I am already dreading my December heat bill.

I don't have a problem with climate change per say. The record of the Earth itself proves that it exists. There is evidence aplenty of periods of glacier activity and periods of ice, where there is now only warmth. I am a little skeptical of it being caused by man. I think of it as naturally occurring. There have always been periods of climate change, and many were beyond man's time. It's my guess there always will be, even when man has departed from the scene. Regardless, I am absolutely positive that I have noticed some pretty good changes in just my life time. All I have to do is think back to those cold

winters of my childhood.

Sinusitus

December is turning out to be a cold one. It's not only a cold month, but it's been a sick one for many. I had to break down after two weeks and make my way to the doctor for serious coughing and sinus issues. Nothing over the counter seemed to help, and when you do try to let these things run their course, it sometimes doesn't work. In my case the coughing was interfering with my sleep, and I was beginning to feel very run down. So, I got some meds, and with crossed fingers am trying.

Why do all the flues, viral infections, colds, etc. predominately seem to take hold during the brief period of the Winter Solstice? I know they are here year around, but this period seems far more prevalent for sickness. Maybe it's all the mingling folks do around those commercial Holidays. New year's is now a big spending time as the big retailers cut inventory to the bone in an effort to unload their leftover Christmas stock.

Maybe it's because we shun the outdoors and fresh cold air so much, and stay in a dry, warm, sealed atmosphere that is perfect for bacteria to thrive once it enters. Then, there is always the dark, cold, bleak days, that December is known for. Could a little shadow of depression that lingers for a few weeks bring our immune systems down?There are studies that says it does, and some of those studies claim it can affect one's physical health in a big way.

This make's two Christmas's in a row that I have been suffering through some kind of virus. Usually of the sinus, head cold, or lungs. Whatever it is, in my case, along with many others, its usually attributed to clogged sinuses that won't drain. I don't recall all these bouts of sickness as a child. I don't ever recall people talking about a virus making the rounds. Oh, I do remember a few old men pulling their hanky, and blowing their noise, with the remark that they had a little cold, but it was only a few.

What I do remember most, was us little kids playing outside, winter, summer, and fall. It was during those winter months, that one could have called us "little snotty nosed kids." There were no problems with clogged sinuses in those days. Our nose ran all the time out in that air, and we were forever blowing and wiping. We were not too particular about what we wiped with either. Caught up in the excitement of our play, we found nothing worked any better than a shirt sleeve. You might say if the bottom of your shirt sleeves were a little stiff during the winter, you were a redneck. Not exactly sanitary, but as I said, our sinuses always drained, and that was probably why we never got sick. They were continuously being flushed out.

Today, at the first sign of drainage, we grab something to dry it up. One cannot have a child with a runny nose, nor would people feel comfortable around a grown-up who was having a little mucus accumulate on his upper lip. Not being a doctor, I can't say, but I'm betting that nasal discharge is a defense mechanism, and that was one reason us children never got sick with all this crap we suffer from today.

Last year when I went through a bout of this infected sinus malady, my doctor prescribed something to dry it up. Then, he sent me for a sinus X-ray, and a few days later advised me that those showed I'd suffered some damage at one time to my nasal structure and bones, which kept them from properly draining. Therefore, he recommended surgery. I of course declined as I have had friends who did that, and it did not help. At least in their case. Besides it's a very uncomfortable and painful deal., Unless they have improved on it from several years back when it first became the fad.

No, I am too old now, and have lived with the Sinus issue for so long that I will try to struggle on through. I take a peek in our Medicine cabinet now and then. It bothers me somewhat to see all the allergy medicines, the cough syrups, the Claritin, the nasal sprays, with the name of my little eight-year-old Granddaughter attached. I don't approve of running to the doctor every time one gets the sniffles, but that is pretty much the norm now.

Anyway, back to my case. Should I have had surgery, and my sinuses had started running again, it's a sure bet my doctor would have said, we need to give you something to dry up that sinus discharge. So, who really knows what's cool now? I have had issues all my life with sinuses, but it's only in my olden years that I have come to realize how really sick they can make you. Sinuses can, and will, often put an older person down for a day or several weeks.

And as for the damage done to my nasal structure noticed by X-Ray, well that occurred sometimes in the mid-sixties, and I had problems before, and problems since, so, I can't blame a few former broken bones. I do wish that old Bosum mate hadn't hit me so hard just for dancing with his girl. Though, it did much more damage to my pride than did the broken nose, at least back then. In the later years, the broken nose came back to haunt me, and now won't let my sinuses drain.

Hog Killing

The old fashion hog killings have gone the way of most other mountain traditions. You very seldom see one being carried out at home. The vast majority of people only know that you go to some chain grocery and buy your meat already processed and packed. They give little thought to the existence of the animal prior to its placement into the roaster.

There are still a few around that like to raise their own meat animals, but even those opt out of home slaughtering, and carry them to a commercial slaughter house to be killed and processed. Then, when they go back for pick up, the meat is neatly packed, and labeled as to the different cuts, etc., and is freezer ready. A very neat and efficient way to handle your home raised beef or hogs, and with a very minimum of labor involved.

It wasn't too many years back that most families in rural Owsley County killed and processed their own meat, and that being primarily hogs. My family, like most others on Buffalo was no exception. As recently as fifty and sixty years ago it was a family tradition, and hog killing time was a highly anticipated and looked forward to affair. At least that is the way us kids saw it, and we were forever in the way and were always being yelled at and chased away from the work area. An area that could be dangerous because of sharp instruments, scalding water, and the hanging of the hogs.

We were mostly hanging out to grab the first fresh piece of meat available. When we got that small piece of lean meat, we stuck it quickly onto a sharpened stick, and headed to the fire place where we roasted it until it turned brown and dripped with grease. Then we ate what was one of the tastiest treats one could imagine. Now, I don't know anything about hog killing, as my many hours of observing was as a child, and instead of helping I was mainly in the way. However, there are still several hardy individuals I know who still prefer the old-time method. When I get a chance or an invite to drop by on that particular day, I usually try to go. To me it brings back good memories, and it's also like watching local history on replay. On top of that, I have never saw a hog killing that someone didn't fry up a little of that lean meat before the process was over. So, one can observe and enjoy some of the fresh kill. I don't know why but the meat will never again taste as good as it does when its freshly killed.

Us kids in my days found this activity enjoyable to observe, but I'd guess today they would be a little grossed out. Just a few days back Buster Viries, Gary Deaton, and a few others were killing on the Left Fork. Thankfully, I was invited, and of course I went, and I am glad I did. As I said earlier, I know little about the methods and knowledge of this mountain tradition, but you can't watch it done by folks like this without learning. As a child I never noticed the details, but with these guys you notice there is a method, or procedure, even an art of sorts you might say. A system that has been used, and continues to be, since the first old settlers drove their hogs through the Cumberland Gap. I watched those guys go through the steps.

I remembered my father always laid his hog out on a large board and then poured hot water on it as he scraped, but this crew used a tank of hot water whereby the entire hog was lifted and dipped into that tank, and a hoe was used for scraping. I had never saw the hoe used before. Of course, prior to that, the hog had been killed and hung for a brief period to bleed. Following that, it was raised from the tank and hung for finish scraping, cleaning, washing, rinsing. Etc. then follows the gutting and beheading. Now, it's not my intention to walk one through every step, but I am merely pointing out that there is a procedure, and to give one that has never saw this, some general idea.

Everything has to be done right, and even the temperature of the weather has to be agreeable for this activity. When you place that hog into the hot water for scraping, the water temperatures have to be right also, as you don't want to boil the layers of skin. You just want it hot enough so the hair will come loose. So, there is knowledge needed. The Hogs Killed in my youth had no waste products except the intestines, and those were stripped of any fat which was rendered into lard. I have noticed that the modern-day slaughters dispose of certain parts that we would have never dreamed of throwing away. The heads, feet, tail, interior parts such as lungs, tongue, liver, kidneys, heart, etc. now mostly get discarded.

Those parts were highly sought in the old days. Us kids always roasted the kidney's first thing. The nose was always sought out by my mother who prepared it and then baked it. I remember it as being quite delicious. In those days too, the day after the killing and processing, was dedicated to the rendering of the fat. Thus, assuring a good supply of lard being on hand.

I appreciate getting to watch Buster, Gary, and the others. A very efficient crew they were. I got to thinking about some things after I left. Some talk I heard while observing as a young boy in those long-gone days of yore. I recalled there were some people who believed you should only kill by the sign of the moon. Others swore you never killed a hog on a new moon. Others believed you killed on a full moon. Much like the old timers who went by the signs to plant crops, many went by the moon signs, believing that certain signs of the moon impacted the meat and by products such as lard production. I wanted to ask Buster and Cap about that but they were much too busy, so I will inquire the next time we meet.

As I said, I did not help any as they seemed to have plenty on hand, and I'd probably been more in the way than anything. However, I did help keep the plate clean of the fresh fried meat, which was a task more agreeable to me. More than anything though, I am thankful to those fresh fried ribs, and the grease on my chin as I sit here at the table tonight. I am also reminded by that grease, that one of the statements I put forth above was not exactly correct. The intestines were not always discarded, especially as it related to the small ones. There were some who cut the small intestines up and cleaned them well, then fried. The byproduct of that was called chitterlings (pronounced Chit-Lins). An all-time southern favorite.

Greg Shouse – Owsley County Hog Killing 2017

Rattlesnake Childhood – by Carol Dean Moore

I am thankful that God saw it fit for my paternal grandparents to raise me, from a little one year old to what I turned out to be. They instilled in me the values that I have to this day. God had given them ten children of their own and knew they would do well with this one. They would have been well into their years when they took another little child to feed and clothe, and to raise the way she should be. It meant several more years of hard work, but they did not mind that. I was taught to work, at home as well as in the garden, and also in the corn and tobacco patches.

I didn't mind the work, it was just something that had to be done. I always liked it when, in the winter time, I would find a hen egg that was frozen, as I knew that meant I would get to eat that egg for supper. Always loved gathering the eggs and finding a fresh batch of little chickens that had just hatched. There were always many things to keep me busy. I was allowed to take Old John, our old mule, out for his evening exercise. This old mule was so gentle. We always had cats around, everyone for miles around must have known that I would find any cat that was dropped anywhere near our house. One time a momma cat had her kittens in Grandma's meal barrel. It must have been a sight, could have been funny if it was not so serious. A sack of meal was not easy to come by in those days. I don't remember if Grandpa took another load of corn to the mill to be ground, or if he had to buy a bag of, as he called it, "that old, bolted meal", which he did not have an appetite for. But all in all, they must have tolerated most of the cat happenings.

I remember once when Ed and Ollie Dean and their family moved off of Buffalo Creek to Northern Ky. Ollie wrote me a letter that they had left a white cat behind and that I could have it if we would go down and get it. Grandma and I went down to their old house and brought Snowball home with us. That was one happy kid!

I am sure this kid caused them many a worry, but somehow, we all survived it. I have many happy memories of growing up on the Rattlesnake Branch. Maybe more to come later. Hope some of you enjoyed this memory.

George Barrett: Kentucky's Meanest Man?

The Period of the late 1920's and 1930's was a hard time for America. There were few jobs and little money to be had, so some people took the easy way out and turned to a life of crime.

A new type of criminal was in vogue. Gangs of young farm boys roared their high-powered vehicles throughout the country; robbing, killing, and doing whatever else struck their fancy. These were men such as Dillinger, Barrows, "Baby Face" Nelson, and many others. There were infamous women as well such as Bonnie Parker, "Ma" Barker, and others.

The automobile transformed the way crime was done in America. These gangsters were highly mobile. They could hit in one state, and in hours or minutes be in another.

They were a different breed. Most, if not all, came from hardworking farm families. They defied the traditional image of a criminal, as there were seldom any previous convictions of family members or other associates.

They were a nightmare for peace officers, but to the general public that felt hunger pains, they sort of took on the appearance of modern-day Robin Hoods. Later, they became known as the "Hayseed Killers," primarily because of their rural roots.

Local and state law enforcement officials could not cope with this new breed, so a new federal agency was pressed into service. The FBI, or "G-men," as they were called, knew no state boundaries and were quickly getting the upper hand. Under the direction of young John Edgar Hoover, the FBI was merciless in its pursuit. Its agents would set an ambush, yell out "F-B-I," then fire their weapons, all in the same instant. In the 1930's, this proved to be a highly-effective tactic.

J. Edgar Hoover, leading the forefront and often on site at every engagement, rode a wave of publicity to infamy. He proudly boasted that he himself was involved in every major case. He accepted an offer and did a series of stories for the American Magazine in the 1930's. In the May, 1937 issue he did a story called "The Meanest Man I Ever Knew." The director didn't give that distinction to Dillinger or any other from the more famous Hayseed gangs. Instead, that dubious distinction went posthumously to Clay County, Kentucky Native George Barrett.

Hoover was known to be somewhat boastful, but by no means was he ever considered a liar. The fact is that in the early years of the FBI he kept close tabs on all the high-profile criminal cases. He also learned and knew many "mean men."

While George Barrett was, in fact, a "gentlemen gangster" of some repute, it is doubtful that he is the meanest man Hoover ever had to deal with. George was born in the peaceful little valley of Crane Creek in Clay County Kentucky, ca. 1887. His parents were William and Nancy Bowling Barrett.

The family appears to have moved from Clay to Jackson County ca. 1900. William allegedly removed his family from the area in an attempt to protect them from the Baker, Howard, and White troubles that were beginning to brew. If this was the case, it did little to improve Georges' lot in life. He seemed to have an early inclination for trouble and lawlessness.

Early on, he acquired a glass eye, because of a shootout with his brother-in-law.

In 1913 he lost a round with U.S. Marshal C.T. Nickells, while making moonshine. He served a little prison time for it, but it did nothing to change his path of crime.

George became a true gangster later in life. He spent much of his time in the St. Louis, Missouri; and Cincinnati, Ohio areas. Occasionally he slid into Eastern Kentucky to hide among his friends. He loved flashy cars, pretty women, and carrying a wad of green. In some way or another, he always seemed to be in possession of all three.

In the underworld he became known as the "Diamond King," and word was out that if you wanted to buy real diamonds cheaper than wholesale, he was the man to see.

Barrett discovered there was a lot of money to be made in nice automobiles. He perfected a system of changing serial numbers and creating paperwork that would make any car instantly legal. Thus, he became involved in interstate auto theft throughout the Midwest.

George married five women and lived with many more. He fathered four legitimate children and had several others who were illegitimate.

Hoover claimed that George was a major firearms supplier to the underworld. This is not unlikely, since he served three different times in the military and had the connections to acquire stolen military arms. He used the military as a training academy to acquire proficiency in firearms. He became an expert of many different weapons, and at each enlistment he bought himself out, whenever he felt his need had been met. Strangely enough, stamped on his military papers are the words "excellent character."

The military training must have worked, because it was rumored within the criminal element that you didn't want to get into a shootout with George Barrett. He himself bragged that he had killed at least six men. Hoover concurred by stating that Barrett had murdered several.

We don't know of all the evil deeds of Kentucky's most notorious gangster. But his life was full of surprises. It required extensive writing to cover what is already known about him. There is a wealth of information, as he left quite a paper trail in marriages, divorces, military records, criminal dossiers, and many old newspaper accounts from the mid-1930's. However, it seemed that J. Edgar Hoover wrote the article in American Magazine in 1937 because of two highly-publicized crimes.

In 1930 George came to visit his six-year-old son in Jackson County, who was being looked after by his 71-year-old grandmother. The child told his father of some punishment he'd received from his grandmother. An argument followed, and in a fit of rage, George pulled his gun and shot his mother to death.

Georges sister, Rachel, tried to intercede but was pistol-whipped. Making her escape, she ran and jumped into a passing mail truck. George fired at the truck, striking

Rachel in the head. She later died of medical complications, while being treated for her wounds.

George continued his criminal enterprises, while the law sought him with no results. Then, in 1931, he sent word to his friends in the mountains that he was coming home to stand trial and clear himself. He had the money and a cousin who was the prosecutor.

Barrett kept his word. The first trial ended in a mistrial, but George was acquitted in the second trial. Frank Baker had put up such a shabby prosecution that the judge scolded him in open court, accusing him of doing more to defend than prosecute the defendant.

Gun hands were in demand, at that time, so Frank Baker took on cousin George as a sharp shooting bodyguard. However, this failed to save Bakers life. He and another bodyguard, John Brockman, died during a wall of gun fire as they crossed the street at the Clay County Courthouse.

Again, Barrett's luck held. Sensing something was wrong just seconds before the shooting, he drew his guns and dived under an automobile. He shouted the alarm to Baker, but it was too late. The car had sixteen bullet holes in it, but none of them found George.

The incident never changed George, as his free-willing ways continued. He again became a wanted man, and his love of guns, diamonds and automotive enterprises continued to flourish.

One sultry, hot summer night in the little town of College Corners, Indiana, he

heard the call, "F-B-I," George went for his gun and dropped behind a tree. FBI agent

Nelson B. Klein died from a barrage of five bullets from Barrett's gun. His partner lived,

however, and wounded Barrett in the legs, which crippled him for the rest of his life.

George Barrett, the feudist, gangster, murderer and mountain Casanova, was

finally in the clutches of J. Edgar Hoover. A few months earlier, a new federal law went

into effect making the killing of a federal peace officer a capital offense. When George

chose to shoot it out with the FBI and killed one of their agents, he sealed his own fate.

A spectacular trial followed, capturing the focus of the entire nation, not to

mention much local interest. George needed a colorful attorney who was also a

staunch mountaineer. Edward Everett Rice, formerly of Owsley County, rose to the

occasion.

At Barrett's trial Rice portrayed Barrett as a victim. He argued that George

thought he was being attacked by his feudal enemies from the Kentucky mountains. He

also angered many by referring to the FBI as "little boys playing as being cops."

However, the jury returned with a verdict of "guilty," and federal judge Robert C.

Baltzell did what he had never done before in his 40 years on the bench. He sentenced

a man to death by hanging.

Indiana geared up for Georges execution. According to all of the major news

sources of that time, Barrett remained calm and collected, until the very end. He had

lived with reporters throughout the trial and developed a camaraderie with many of

them.

After thanking the jail staff and reporters, and even informing his executioner that he had no animosity towards him or anyone else, he was carried to the scaffold, at 12:01 a.m., March 24, 1936. Still crippled from the FBI agent's bullets, he was held upright until the trap door could be sprung.

Ironically, his last words before ascending the ladder were, "Gentlemen, I am ready to go be with my mother."

Hoover immediately sent personal congratulations to the prosecutor, Val Nolin.

How mean did Hoover think George Barrett really was? Let's look at the early records. John Dillinger, Bonnie and Clyde, and other gangsters of the era were ambushed and gunned down; usually, with Hoover present. It would seem that Barrett was so dangerous and difficult to capture, the FBI certainly would have sent in more than just two agents. He would never have been given the opportunity to fire his gun.

J. Edgar Hoover was a master of records and details. He may have known more about George Barrett than what came to light during the trial. He knew that George lived under at least six aliases during his lifetime, and he probably knew how many people George had killed.

It really isn't important whether George Barrett was the meanest man in Kentucky. He was a product of his time, growing up around various feuds. He turned bad in his youth and never altered that course. There were many others like him, during this period of history, but he chanced to catch more of the publicity.

www.ingramcontent.com/pod-product-compliance
Lightning Source LLC
Chambersburg PA
CBHW081305250726
48662CB00008B/2408